The Plumbline, By Timothy Lane Trull, Sr.

Builders have used a plumbline for thousands of years to ensure the walls on a building are straight. God gave us the Bible to help us keep our lives straight. Often, we ignore the tenants, and that is when we start building crooked walls within our lives. Focus on the fundamentals of the Bible, and rebuild your life in a straight line. The Plumbline is a book written for anyone that may benefit from this one sinners walk through life, finding a nearly straight line after so many years.

The days of being prejudiced against blacks, Asians, Hispanics, whites, or other races are gone. Today, men and women that work are prejudice against men and women who are not willing to work, and take free subsidies illegally and immorally from those that work. The time has come for all men and women to step up to the plate for this country, and to start working toward making our nation profitable again.

We had national pride when we were a moral nation. Overlooking corruption of political and business leaders, lying companies, unethical stock brokers, pornography, excessive usury, free credit, 3rd generation welfare.....we have destroyed ourselves. Lets go back to the basics... a honest days work for an honest days pay. And, a system of Justice that really gives justice to the victim.

The following page is the bottom line up front; I want to motivate people to:

--Post the 10 Commandments in your house, read them every morning, ask for forgiveness immediately after breaking one. Do every thing possible to do all of them, including Honoring the Sabbath.

--Do unto others as you would have them do unto you.

Also:

1. Pray

2. Read the Bible completely through reading 5 pages a day.

3. Fast for 4 hours at a time.

4. Eat Biblically. Read Exodus and do it no matter what others say.

5. Understand lust is in the mind, and is adultery, even looking. Ask daily for forgiveness.

6. Turn off the television.

7. Go to a church of your choice once a week.

8. Love your spouse and children.

9. Forgive. Forgive everyone. Pray for your enemies and those who might harm you.

10. Do 1 nice thing for someone every day. Mow someone else's yard. Bake a cake for your neighbor.

11. Tithe 10% (+) to your church.

12. Read Psalms 91 everyday.

13. Have your children memorize Psalms 23 and the Lords Prayer.

14. Sit quietly after prayer and wait for the Lords answer. Remember, your prayer should be about the will of God and not our own will. For example, if your job is requiring you to work on the Sabbath, this may be against the will of God as one of his Commandments was to Obey the Sabbath, and keep it Holy. But, pray about it and wait. Grow where you are planted. If God wants you changed, he will change it.

15. Don't gossip.

16. Obey all laws. Even speed limits.

17. Go and visit shut ins, injured, and diseased.

18. Make an anonymous donation to a homeless shelter or homeless church.

19. Call your parents, brothers and sisters, and other family at least weekly.

20. Do things to make someone else successful at work. Work at making someone else rich.

21. Plant a garden and can vegetables. Buy meat from local butchers. The scientific fast feeding of

animals and plants may cause future health problems and animal problems. I.e.: Turkeys can no longer have sex amongst themselves to reproduce because their chests are too big from chemical growth. Google it. What other changes to plants and animals are we making??

22. Pay cash for all you can, or if possible, barter. Do a service for something.

23. Help the Police catch criminals. Be involved in your Community Watch.

24. Help someone going down the wrong path without judging them. Many criminals would not be criminals if they could find a job. Give people a 2nd chance.

Consider asking your Congress Representative and Senators the following:

1. Law Enforcement needs to know who is the owner of each vehicle. Liberal 30 day laws and dealer tag laws help hide criminal's identity. We need to have a law enacted to where each dealer when they sell a car automatically registers the vehicle to the new owner by computer. And, individuals who sell cars must take the buyer to the Department of Motor Vehicles for transfer of ownership. People break laws and commit crimes daily and hide who they are by driving vehicles with fake tags.

2. Fight allowing Gay people to marry. Read the story of Sodom and Gomorrah again and see if it sounds familiar. We are almost there.

3.   Fight enacting laws to legalize drug use
(marijuana, etc.). These drugs are commonly

in the possession of criminals, and the more
available it becomes, the more criminals we will
have in the US. We have enough.

4.   We need a 4 strikes and you are out provision,
especially with violent crimes. We do not need to
continue housing violent criminals who hurt
someone and go to jail, get out of jail, hurt someone,
go to jail, get out of jail, kill someone, go to jail, get
paroled, kill someone else, go to jail, ...why
could we not send these individuals to Somalia or
some other 3rd world country away from law
abiding Americans if we don't agree on the death
penalty? Also, corrupt politicians. If someone we
have elected gets convicted of a corruption or
immoral crime while in public office, they need to be
voted off the island. There has to be a way we can
take away US citizenships as freely as we have been
giving them away.

5. Pray for wisdom and understanding about voting.
Then go out and vote. Then pray again. There are I
believe some God led men still in politics. I believe
very strongly in Lindsey Graham from SC.

6. Write your Congressman or Senator about
starting a fund for Americans who want to donate
cash to get America out of debt. For about $980 per
American we can once again become debt free. The
National Debt is a tremendous threat on our
National Security. This is one thing the Secretary of
State, Hillary Clinton understands. Why don't the
rest?

7. Plan for taking care of your parents when they get older. We can take care of our families without government assistance.

8. Pray for God's wisdom in decision making when dealing with the worldly circumstances at hand. No intelligent or moral person will support burning the Koran or other religious materials. But if we let and support the government stepping in to stop it, then we are supporting the abolition of the 1st Amendment. Few American's believe the right place to build a Mosque is at the World Trade Center site, as it was taken down and thousands of Americans killed by Muslim extremists. But if we say as a government "you can't build here", the government is no longer allowing freedom of religion. We need intelligent, thoughtful, prayerful men and women in government that can see through the attacks of our Constitution and can articulate the forefather's intentions. The Constitution, Declaration of Independence, and other works of our founding fathers are more than works by common men....they are works that are inspired by God.

Make your politicians support the Constitution, or make them resign. A political term may be for 2 years, but when they suck at their job....it may be time to go. Why do we hold onto what is failing?

We are on the brink of giving up the freedoms that our forefathers fought hard for us to possess. As the next generation sells off to foreigners that by which their parents and grandparents built, the common man becomes one step closer to losing their freedom. After all, when we are all dependent on the government, or a government for our livelihood, then we will all become slaves to our stomachs. The pattern of government we are destroying is damaging to all. Even the wealthy seller of a business overseas risks becoming a slave to another. Do you really think a government in need of money will overlook your money in a bank? Wake up. We need God more than ever and as you allow this need and obligation to be dismissed, the US becomes 1 step closer to becoming a Socialist Country. Re-dedicate yourselves, your family and your wealth to Christ. It is the only way to not only save yourselves, but to save all of us. Then, work to make yourself self-sufficient, paying taxes to the government and obeying its laws, but depending on it for nothing. By ourselves, we cannot do this. With God, all things are possible. Re-dedicate your lives and future to God, and your salvation to his son, Jesus Christ.

To do this, start with yourself. Walk a straight line and path, so others may follow.

Simon the Just, a high priest who is praised in the book Ecclesiastics, once stated, "The World Rests on Three Things, on the Law, on Divine Service, and on Charity."

Lets restore our country and our world using that which is tried and true; The Bible, Prayer and Hard

Work. Also, start or support small manufacturing business (wood, furniture, linen, etc.) or other service related business that is being taken over by foreign countries. Finally, teach your children the importance and how to work hard. Our next generation is going to be way behind the Chinese and other countries because we don't work hard.

Tim Getner was amazed when he ran for and won a position as a US Senator in 2014. After all, he had never ran for a political position before; nor accomplished much of anything with his life before for that matter. You see, he was not the type of person who usually wins a political election. Of middle class background, a small business owner (he cut grass and painted for a living), quiet, seemingly honest, and with few friends. He was the type normally overlooked for political office.

But, this year, he hit a goldmine. He ran on the proposition of sending 4th time convicted criminals to Somalia for the rest of their lives. For example, a man convicted of shoplifting four times, was shipped to Somalia. A man convicted of four DWIs, was sent to Somalia to drink and drive. A woman who was convicted of possession of crack cocaine four times, could be shipped to Somalia and do all the crack cocaine she wanted for the rest of her life. The four time rule was a hit with all; conservatives and even some liberals. People of all areas of the United States were tired of their homes being broken into and there tax system burdened, and therefore this was a quick fix. (Misdemeanor Traffic

Offenses were omitted from this, but politicians who were convicted of corruption charges even 1 time were included.)

But, there was a minority that wanted to see this law abolished. When it was passed overwhelmingly in 2014, known as the Getner law, many minority groups were very angry. There were many African Americans, for example, who felt this new law was not fair because it was statistically African Americans who previously had been convicted four or more times for the same crime.

However, in reality, whites, blacks, Hispanics, and others were deported in large numbers as they committed their crimes, and got their fourth conviction for the same thing. Most Asians were never deported, because they were the hardest working and least likely ever to commit crimes.

This is the story of the fix of crime in America; providing a new location for criminals who do not want to change, to have an opportunity to perform their crimes in Somalia. Somalia, a great country for criminals of all nations to converge together and commit crimes.

This solution fixed the prison problem as there were less convicts. And, it took care of the habitual prisoners who were always clogging up the court systems throughout America. But, the solution was just missing something. It was not God inspired as the best solutions through time have been...it was man inspired just like the tower of Babylon. A great idea. A great solution from mans perspective. And, a decision that helped fix the economy and the criminal system.   But, was it God inspired........

A prayer for wisdom: It is my prayer to you, oh Lord, that the words I write are not from my insolent pride or trying to make other humans happy, but that they would be words inspired by you, to change this prideful and arrogant nation, to turn their ways back to the Lord, and to understand that all that we have accomplished and all the blessings we have, are inspired by you and have nothing to do with the minds and hands of men. For through you, men are brought to great heights, and at the snap of a finger, men fall from grace. Therefore, let us as a nation and world remember you, live through you, and learn that by which is right.

This is not easy for me to write, and I want to take out a lot of things in this book that make me look bad. But, I am going to leave them in there so perhaps some young person will learn from my mistakes, and not make the same ones I have. It is often said that God places the weak in a position to share with others, so they may be strong.   These words that I write, I want to be fully inspired by God. My goal for writing all of this is that America will fall back on their knees, tear their clothes, and wail for sadness on how we have turned our back on God. I would then ask all to ask for his grace, and beg for forgiveness. For then, our land could be truly healed. For God wants us to ask for forgiveness sincerely, and fix our lives. He gave us a Bible with life instructions (The Plumbline) to keep us straight if we will follow his rules.

We need a blessing, and its not coming in the direction we are heading. And, the solutions we are coming up with about problems are not God led and inspired, but man led. For example, as we dig further into Socialistic programs to create jobs at taxpayer's expense, we dig our country further and further in debt. How will we ever pay off this deficit?

I feel led to write, because I am worried about the unknown that is going on with this nation. I admit I myself have my own problems, as I have failed and failed and failed, and it is only by reading the Bible, prayer, coffee, and the occasional dip of Skoal that seems to keep me moving forward with life. I have failed and continue to fail daily, and it is so often that I mistakenly place my will, in the place of God, even today, after coming to Christ many years ago. As I begin to write this, I am in Iraq, on the third month of what seems to be an eternity of time before I can go back home. I work as a Company Commander for a Brigade Headquarters, and am stuck in this country (Iraq) until next January, 2010. This is my second one year tour to Iraq in about 6 years. By the way, both one year tours are really about 1.5 years, as there is a train up before, and a demobilization process after. It is hard. I have a wife and four kids at home. My family has been split up. My oldest daughter, 15 years old, who I love very much, has moved out of the house and in with my brother in law because she cannot get along with my wife, and she is an Academically Gifted student. She is making bad grades this year. My other daughter, seems to do good, but often I worry about her as she is very sensitive to all this. And my son, who has Dyslexia, is having problems in school. My wife has Multiple Sclerosis and emails me all the time about how her head hurts, and that she has had a stroke or some other illness, and can't walk, and I have a one year old daughter at home with her. I am here, and there is nothing I can do, but pray, to help my family back home. I am in a position of Command, but I often wonder about my own competence to lead, as I think of home so much. I hate war. But, I hate the idea of the freedoms that our forefathers fought for being eroded and whittled to nothing more. I blame terrorists for taking away my own freedom, as I am stuck in Iraq away from my family.

It does not take long to figure out why we are here. The Al Qaeda idiots would kill everyone if we weren't sustaining the power of the Iraqi government and the people. They would send a 6 year old boy unknowingly in with a bomb, to kill one of us or one of the elected officials in the Iraqi government. It is becoming blazingly obvious that we will have to fight Al Qaeda in Iraq, and the Taliban in Afghanistan to the death, as they can only see their pretend Jihad as the solution to their woes. If they could only see that they could accomplish more through the will of God than trying to create their own will. But, they want to be right by themselves instead of with God. This internal struggle inside of man to create his own will in spite of God's will has created most wars and struggles since the beginning of time. Why could they not have a leader who has read history books??

Another reason why we are still here, and I want to believe this, is for the protection of Israel, even in Iraq. There are pro-Hezbollah fighters here, and the United States always has been and always will be obligated to protect Israel. I have a strong belief that we should always have Israel's back, as God has chosen them as his people.   But, even in the Bible there have been times when God turned his back on

Israel, especially when evil rulers and people created policy for the Jewish people. The true Jewish people, who read this I hope might tear their clothes, fall on their knees, and also beg God for forgiveness. For then their land could be truly healed. We all will need God on our side for what we are about to face. Therefore, we must support and recruit God led and filled men, capable of fasting and following the word of God. For they will lead our nation and our world toward safety, and away from the evil. These men should be recruited from all religions, Christians, Jews, Muslims, Buddhists, etc. True Godly men who make decisions after prayer and fasting, and not from their own worldly knowledge.

I think I know why we came in and took out Saddam. I know why we searched for weapons of mass destruction, which were taken out of the Qa Qa Weapons Facility in Baghdad, Iraq before we could get our hands on them (witnesses saw trucks with Conex Boxes of something dumped into the Euphrates River as we pushed into Baghdad at the start of the war). The end was justified. But, at what point will we take out the remaining aggressors. At what point will we get on line with the entire US Military forces in Iraq, and clear the country from the North to the South, stopping in every home and hole in the desert? Then, at what point will we move to Afghanistan and do the same thing? Is this war in line with what the will that God has for our nation?

I will fight for Israel because they are Gods chosen people. However, there may be a time when God chooses them to lose as they have not lived up to the rules and obligations that he set before him in the Torah. I will remain on their side to my own possible demise, as they are the beginning of my past.

God said he will once again bless the Jewish people and nation. But, look at the Jewish bankers and how they charge the poor interest. Or look at the Jewish owned movie producers who produce pornographic material that goes around the world, including onto Arabic satellites for consumption in Muslim homes. Or, what is it that they are doing for widows and orphans around the world? Can you imagine the Muslim father, who is switching through channels as he watches television with his 14 year old daughter; and as he changes channels he runs across two Americans having sex in his home. The pornography industry has done more for the destruction of America and the world in the last 40 years that anything else. And, businessmen and bankers just wink-wink, nod-nod as it creates revenue. Sin sells. There is no way this is the will of God as it goes against everything in the Bible. And, unfortunately pornography helps fuel the hatred Muslims have toward America. Many Muslims truly see us as the great Satan, even after all the help and money we give away.

Antiochus IV Epiphanes

Antiochus IV Epiphanes was a Seleucid ruler over Syria and Israel from 175-163BC, and even ruled Egypt for a short time. Antiochus made it illegal to worship the Jewish religion, burned Israel, and killed multitudes of Jews, as well as got rid of many Jewish observances. On or about December, 167 BC he offered a sow on the altar outside of the temple, a dramatic slap in the face to Jewish people. This caused an uprising and a time period known as the Maccabean revolt. There were three years of fighting before the Jewish people were able to once again restore temple worship around 163BC. This rededication of the temple is still celebrated today as a eight day holiday for Jewish people known as Hanukkah.

Daniel said the following prayer in Daniel Chapter 4, Verse 3-7: And I set my face unto the Lord God, to seek by prayer and supplications, with fasting and sackcloth, and ashes, And I (Daniel) prayed unto the Lord my God and made my confession and said, O Lord, the great and dreadful God, keeping the covenant and mercy to them that love him, and to them that keep his commandments, We have sinned and have committed iniquity, and have done wickedly, and have rebelled, even by departing from thy precepts and from thy judgments. Neither have we hearkened unto thy servants the prophets, which spake in thy name to our kings, our princes, and our fathers, and to all the people of the land. O Lord, righteousness belongeth to thee, but unto us confusion of faces, as at this day to the men of Judah, and to the inhabitants of Jerusalem, and unto all Israel, that are near, and that are far off, through all the countries whither thou hast driven them, because of their trespass that they have trespassed against thee........................

I know Jewish people are blessed because they are of Israel, and God's chosen people, but that still does not make their actions right when they portray that which was given to humans as holy, and throw it to the pigs. Even David in the Bible, when he took it upon himself to conduct a census without God's permission, was punished by God. What punishment does a nation that condones homosexuality, abortion, divorce, adultery, corruption, and lying deserve? Massive hurricanes, and a oil spill in the gulf? Does that begin to show how hard it is to clean our souls from the sins that stains them. The dirt is much dirtier on our souls than taking pig shit and wiping it all over us.

To confuse things more, we as a Christian nation want to give to those who do not have, but in weird ways. For example, the Army gives out $5000 micro grants to families in Iraq or Afghanistan, to help people start small businesses. They call it money as a weapon system. One of the weirdest things about this is that many American Small Business Owners need $5000. Where is their micro grants? Also, and unfortunately, some of this money given is paid to Al Quada by the families we give it to, for protection money. The system we are now using may not be working with these people. If we are going to stay in Iraq, perhaps we should have a military dictatorship under a General and kill people who would dare fight against us or them. We, to wipe out our enemies, could go from South to North and search every house and area, and find any insurgents. Instead, in 2010, with the technology we have, we take it on "chance" or "hope" that the enemy did not put an IED on the road last night, as we travel 30km to hand out a micro grant to a farmer who will probably give half of it as protection money to Al Qaida, just like an episode of the Sopranos. And, our enemy is not really scared of us any more. We are either at war or we are not at war. If we are at war, why do we not kill our enemies? Is that not the will of God?? Why don't we take an operational pause, get the religious leaders of the world together at a quiet place, and have them pray and fast for understanding? Is it because we no longer put any emphasis on what George Washington felt was sacred. "In God We Trust."

We, as Americans, can live with Muslims, as we have invited them in our country. In August 2010 our President has supported the Muslims to even build a mosque near the World Trade Center complexes that were destroyed. This giving, is a fundamental Christian concept, as the Muslims would not allow us to build a Christian Church in Taliban held territory. But, we have given and given and given. If they cannot wake up to the year 2010 and understand that Allah did not decree to kill every person who does not believe just like them, then we need to really go to war against them. So far, we have been playing war. They have never really seen us in action. The US military when it wants to take out a target, is lethal. The upcoming war will be Israel and the United States against the Islamist Fundamentalist, with no micro grants, and no mercy. Just war to end the war. Because the true Islamists will not read their own Koran and say killing for the sake of killing is wrong. The war is coming because Islamic fundamentalists will not lay down their weapons and enter the 21st century. But, is this the will of God? Does God want us to kill one another through nuclear proliferation? Does God want us as a nation to become enslaved financially to the Muslims or another country because we acted on greed on what he gave us?

Making Money

On September 18, 1905 Frank Tilbert created the Continental Shoe Company in Manhattan, New York. In 1905, the economy was not very stable but he kept trying. Frank created his business by making a pair of shoes, then taking his shoes to local businesses and selling them. With the profit from making 1, and then 2 or more shoes, he grew his small business into a small empire. During World War I, Frank became one of the largest suppliers of Patton type dress shoes for the US Army.

Frank was an honest man. His father and mother raised him with a strong regard for the Bible. He went to church on Sunday, and taught Sunday school as well as held a weekly Bible reading class. He understood the need for Christ, and felt it was his greatest gift.

Frank died in 1958, at 78 years old. At the time of his death, he was worth over $1.8 million and had contributed to many churches and community projects in the Manhattan area. In the same year, Frank's son, Roger Tilbert took over the business. Roger was also brought up in the church, and understood the importance of being honest in business. Under his helm, the company continued to grow, and became one of the most prestigious shoe companies in America. Very few people who lived in the 1960s through the 1980s did not own a pair of Continental Shoe Company's Patton leather work shoes, if they worked as a business professional.

Roger through his life was also a great Christian. He gave to his employees, other organizations, and even helped by providing $1,000,000 to Islamabad after a terrible flood that left thousands dead in 1983. Roger died in 1993, and through such gave the helm of his company to his son, Charles. Charles was a little different.

Charles was a worldly sort, who had been all over the world before he turned 20. At 37 when he took over the company, Charles wanted to maximize profit and increase his business like never before. Instead of looking at what was right like the 2 generations before him, his focus was on dealing with accountants and lawyers, to maximize profits and take the company public. In 2003, Charles took the company public. He made millions, and in 2006 became a billionaire. In 2007, he agreed to give over the helm of the company to a Chinese company that offered him $3 billion for the company, and that he would never have to work again. He sold the company, and in 2007, and retired at 54 years old. He immediately began living the life of luxury that only a wealthy man in 2007 could live. He flew around the world. He played golf at every top level course in the world. Life was good. During this time, many other large family owned businesses were sold also.

In 2015, after 8 years of recession and government spending trying to keep the US at a level of income that it had had for years, the US government went broke. The US government claimed all money within all banks and financial institutions, as well as trust funds as theirs. The government immediately claimed Marshall law, with the US Military and National Guard standing as Police Officers throughout the US to ensure that all assets were equally divided amongst all. Everyone could have a $100k house, all could have 2 cars of any kind, and the excess was put in the government reserve. The US government once again functioned as successful, but no one owned small businesses.

The government owned it all. There was little productivity, as the need to work was no longer there.

In 2016 Charles moved into a 2 bedroom house in Phoenix, Arizona. He had $49 in his pocket, and he drove a Toyota Celica. His grandchildren continued to live in Manhattan, in a townhouse, and went to a Public School in Manhattan. He was unable to hide even the smallest asset from the government, who needed his money to pay off the debt they owed to an overseas nation.

Several of our soldiers have now died on this deployment, as they did on our first deployment. And we are just a bunch of civilians called to active duty from America. The first murder of the soldiers of our unit was when our soldiers left a market (a civilian affairs meeting) and they were surprised by an individual with a suicide vest on, which killed three soldiers, wounding more and also killing civilians. These guys (American soldiers) were out visiting to see where they could spread American money to help the local economy, and they died for it. Our second murder was when 4 of our soldiers rode in a HMMVEE to investigate munitions that were spotted by a helicopter in the air, and they were blown up beyond recognition and burned by 2 x 155mm rounds that exploded under their vehicle. The next murder of our soldiers was an Air Force soldier who was assigned to us as he was travelling South in Baghdad was blown up by a Electromagnetic bomb. We are here trying to rebuild Iraq, giving money to people and helping the average citizen have water and power, and some idiots are out shooting at the same hand that feeds them. And, for what? For some geo-political bullshit so thick, you can cut it. The people in government are so corrupt in Iraq to where it would take 80 years of re-education on how to be ethical in business and life, to where they could come close to running a government like America. And, as you read in the newspaper every morning, we have some wicked and corrupt son of bitches in our government also. So, multiply the corruption in the US government by 25, and you have the level of corruption in Iraq.

So, as you can see, my attitude has to have work daily just to be around other people. And, for the most part, I don't do even a good job with this, as I rarely hang around friends, and would probably be on the bottom 10 of most friendly people. I just chew my tobacco, and keep my mouth shut so that I can function properly. I probably should have read "How to Win Friends and Influence People," but at this juncture of my life, who cares.   As Jesus so eloquently put it, " No man can serve two masters: for either he will hate the one, and love the other; or he will hold to the one , and despise the other." I live it brother. And, our superiors live it as they have to fall under both military and civilian controls during what is supposed to be war? But, my weakness and poor feelings are wrong. I, who wants to be a Christian so badly, fail daily as I feel victimized by this war also. Perhaps it is the will of God and not man that I am sitting in Iraq? After all, we are doing good work here.

There is one thing that I have, and will have it with me when I die. No matter how I feel and how low I am or have been, I have always had Christ with me. He has been my rock and my salvation through the low times and continued low times of life. He lifts me up when humans kick me back down and spit on me. When others would not talk to me, he was there, even when I would not speak to him. I have turned my back on him, questioned him, rejected him, disputed him, lied to him, and knowingly would have been one of the bystanders watching as he was hung on the cross, afraid to say or do anything. And he knows this. Yet, he loves me for some reason. And, he protects me. Last deployment (2004), I had an IED hit between my vehicle and one behind me. He was watching. It only busted the light out on the vehicle behind me. And, there was an IED that was in the ground that I missed as we convoyed by, and before we could come back to check on it, someone (the enemy) had picked it up and took it off to discover why it did not blow up. It did not detonate for a reason that I know, but someone else would not believe. It is like every time I would get in a vehicle and start convoying and look up, I would see a bird flying with me. That was a sign that was only between myself and my maker, and no one else would believe me so I never talk about it. But, it was there.

So, God has watched out for me here. The only reason that I can think of why he would protect me, a sinner, is that he loves me. In fact, he loves me so much he gave me Jesus. This is most evident in the Bible in John 3:16, where it says "For God so loved the world, that he gave his only begotten son, that whosoever believeth in him, should not perish, but have everlasting life. For God sent not his son into the world to condemn the world, but that the world through him might be saved. He that believeth in him is not condemned: but he that believeth not is condemned already, because he hath not believed in the name of the only begotten Son of God." I am writing this before the end of my deployment, and I could easily be killed before the end. But, I believe that if I am, my work on earth was done. And if I am not, God still has some purpose for me that perhaps, I do not understand. (I survived and redeployed back to the US on February 1, 2010. I came closer to getting killed in a car wreck on August 8, 2010 on Bragg Blvd near Highway 87 in my Police Car than I ever did in Iraq).

As a very weak and stubborn man, I stutter, fall, curse, and forget. Yet, no matter where I end up, I will go to heaven because I believe. I am not saying that I do not question, forget, fall, act poorly, and fail. I am just saying through all of my failures and misfortunes, I believe. And, I trust completely in Jesus for my salvation because it is my free gift. I accept the free gift that God has given me, because it is the only sure thing in this world beside taxes.

The Solution

On February 12, 2013 Frank Tillman came up with a great idea. He had been looking for a job for 2 years with no luck, and had no money. He had borrowed every cent possible on every credit card that he and his wife had. His wife and 3 children had now moved in a home in Wilmington, Delaware with her father. Frank was too proud for that. He was getting ready to lose his home and his cars and everything else; but he still had his pride. He was not about to lose that. He had a plan. Taking a last sip from a bottle of bourbon, he got into his 2008 Honda Civic and pulled onto Raeford Rd. heading toward Loris, Delaware. Frank could not remember the last time he was sober, but that would not matter now. He was about to get the money he needed and he would pay back everyone he had ever borrowed from. For the first time in a long time, he was actually hopeful.

His plan was this; he would drive to and park behind the building at 2504 Raeford Rd., which was a semi-abandoned building. He would then walk up the road near the State Employees Credit Union. He would then run into the State Employees Credit Union, demand everyone get down on the floor, and get all the tellers to put the money in bags. He would then run back to his car, through the back yards and woods that would hide him running. He would then get in his car and drive off. It was such a good plan. No one would be hurt, as he would not even load his gun. He would get money so he could get his family back.

The plan started off great. He parked his car and made it to the back of the State Employees Credit

Union without being spotted. He put his mask on, and started into the bank branch. He ordered all people on the floor, and for the tellers to put the money in the bag. He pointed the gun around the room at everyone, to ensure they stayed on the floor. What he did not count on, was a 9mm packing, truck driver, who he accidentally overlooked. When Frank turned his back on the truck driver, he (the truck driver) stood up and pointed the gun at Frank. Frank did not even have his gun loaded, as he was surprised at the interruption, and wanted to ensure up front that no one was hurt. Frank yelled at the truck driver, "put down your gun" and he pointed his unloaded gun at the truck driver. As he pointed in the truck driver's direction, the truck driver took 3 shots from his loaded Glock model 23, putting 3 shots in a triangle shape around Frank's heart. Frank died immediately. All of the patrons of the bank congratulated the truck driver and yelled "hooray." The local television crews were outside, ready to put the "hero" on the news who saved all the people in the bank.

Three days later, Frank was buried in a cemetary in the back of the church he was brought up in. Frank's 7 year old son helped serve as a pall bearer. The members of Frank's father in laws church all donated money to have his funeral. The Pastor, who had known Frank since he was a child but had not seen him in years, tried to think of consoling words for Frank's wife and children over the loss of their father. There was seemingly no answers or words. He wanted to quote Psalms 23, but the words did not seem right. He kept thinking, "why would a man, live so far from the will of God, just because he was going to lose material possessions......" The pastor wound up completing the funeral in silence.

Chapter 1: Introduction

As I have said before, I have been called to write for several years. I start writing for God, and the next thing I know I am adding bits and pieces here and there that have nothing to do with what God initially wanted me to write about. The fact that I am starting this over again, for the third time, has much to do with the fact that I have let pride and arrogance go previously into my words, writing from what I think man would want to hear instead of what man needs to hear. And, from the beginning of man, that pride dooms failure. For many years, God has led my life. When I live right, he blesses me with peace and relative financial soundness. I have and never will get everything I want, but God is the loving father and I know that he is there to protect me. As Psalms 23 says, "thou preparist a table for me in the presence of mine enemies, " and he always has. But, when I let pride and insolence rule my life, he punishes and chastises me so I never forget that everything I own, everything I have, my family, my food, my job, my home, my telephone, my business, is given to me through him, and can as easily be taken away. Our country is the same way.

God gave us the land, the means to prosperity, the gold, the coal, the goodness of the sea. And, as we turn our back on him and think we can do it ourselves, he slowly destroys it, as he did Sodom and Gomorrah. We keep blaming the valve on the oil spill in the gulf. God is in charge of all, good and evil. God is the all seeing eyes and ears of the world, and to those who belong to him, he will guide them and protect them as long as they will turn from their wicked ways. This goes for Israel, Syria, Iraq, Iran, Russia, China, Japan, the United States; everywhere. As Napoleon Bonaparte once said, "the moral is to the physical, as 3:1." This means, if you are morally right against a country who is morally wrong, then you have 3:1 odds. Most US leaders have known this, and have lived Godly lives, and have been blessed to leadership by that which is right. But, God always has and always will place the wicked also in positions of leadership. God uses both good and evil to accomplish his will. And, ultimately that is why we live; to not accomplish our will, but for the fulfillment of his will. For, from the very beginning, the snake existed and God was in control of it. The snake beguiled Eve to eat from the tree, and to get Adam to eat from the tree. God punished the snake to always have to crawl on its belly and to be at enmity between itself and man. No matter what you ever read, know that God is in charge of both good and evil. However, the snake got there before God did when Eve was tempted. The next time you are tempted, pray to God and get him there. He will intervene for you.

I am the son of a banker who worked many of his years for different banks. He also for many years, to make additional income, worked the night shift at a motel so my family could live better. My mother primarily stayed at home. They both worked very hard, raising myself and my two brothers. Growing up in the seventies had much of the strains of today. Gas prices and inflation was rising far faster than salaries. Everyone competed to have what everyone else had. People worked hard to raise families, and people still knew what right and wrong was. I worked hard to be the best at baseball and running. Fred Kirby and the Lone Ranger, two good guys, were on television. And, people overall wanted to see good win. When World Wide Wrestling was on television, kids would pull for the good guy. There was talk of homosexuality, but that was in California. Where I lived we would have none of that. Most of us fully believed that the sins of California would eventually cause it to fall off into the ocean, burn to the ground, or disappear in an earthquake. The Vietnam War was just over, and people were tired of war. They just wanted our soldiers out, and most had no clue why we were in there in the first place.

From the beginning, I should have known I was under God's watchful hand. Other kids could do wrong and get away with it. I was always the one that got caught. Other kids would go out drinking and have huge parties with alcohol. And, the first time I went out drinking with friends, I got drunk and in trouble. I could not hide sin because the all knowing eye was watching, and reporting in to my mother. Some people will laugh. But if you are underneath the eye, you know what I am talking about.

Our country, the United States of America, as a whole, knows what I am talking about. We have a God given obligation as a strong nation to feed the hungry. We have a God given obligation to take care of the weak, and to protect the innocent. If you are American and you question this, then you are not a true American. Take a trip to Washington, DC and look at the influence that God had on our founding fathers. For the true American's, from the beginning, were Christians. This faith from the beginning of our country is what is the driving force to our continued success. As the all knowing eye is on the back of the dollar bill, along with the words, "In God We Trust," so were the words in the founder's eyes. If you question me, which many will, get a copy of the Declaration of Independence and read it again for the first time. Look at how fast we responded to Haiti when the earthquake struck at the early part of 2010. Our country has an internal compass of right and wrong. And, as the Bible says, he who is given much, much will be expected of him.

As I have gotten gotten older, I have come to realize that our country is obligated, just like a human, to God. Within our fabulous system of government, we have built so many checks and balances, to where those highest up in our government cannot get away with things. And, this is right. As the all knowing eye is on our dollar bill, it is also over the Washington Monument. Look at Watergate: sin exposed by the media. Look at Bill Clinton and Monica (as much as it makes me cringe to think about), the media exposed sin. Look at Tianmen Square, Cambodia, and so many other places to where we were forced to act because the media exposed wrongs. Look at the Governor of South Carolina, and so many other high, proud people who are brought low because they are better than others.

Look at the sham election that the Iranian Government had in 2009. Even with televisions and internet shut off, we have "Twitter" that exposes sin. Look at the mountain that Iran has called I believe Qom. They are hiding Nuclear ambitions under a mountain of dirt, near this holy city. This nuclear ambitions could kill thousands of people. Yet, what do they say: we are building nuclear technology for peaceful means. The truth will come out, especially in our current age. And, we must be pressed to act on this truth as we do not need to have our crazy enemy holding nuclear weapons. They will kill a million people and say it was for Allah, and hide while they do it. Our next generation cannot afford us to allow the military dictatorship of Iran to hold a Nuclear Weapon.

Yes, man created Twitter, which keeps us informed about all kinds of happenings all over the world. But, often, man is inspired by God, whether good or evil. No matter what people say about CNN, the Christian Science Monitor, the Jerusalem

Post, Al-Jazeera, and other news media, their work helps to keep freedom of speech alive, and helps to right wrongs which are portrayed through the world. Bad news sells, so people are forced in many cases to stay honest or stink on television and in front of the world. I think God wanted America to be that way, as he spoke to the hearts of the men who wrote the Constitution, giving us Freedom of Speech and a Right to Bear Arms.

God still knows who we are. He blesses us today as he blessed lands before us. And, he will make us suffer as payment for our sins as he made men before us. God gave us men who wrote the United States Constitution, which has constantly been under attack by liberals and hypocrites. However, no matter what you say about our government, there is nothing that beats it in the world. And, people die off the coast of Miami and on the borders of Mexico everyday to get within the border of the United States. Here lately, they have to float through both ocean water and oil to get here, but they are coming.

In October 2009, I went out on a Humanitarian mission to deliver food to Iraqis in Baghdad. We were not far from the base, but it was amazing the amount of impoverished people who came out when we started handing out food. This looked like a junk yard, full of trash, debris from the war, old cars, rusty pipes, etc. But women and children, lived in the middle of this rubble. As we handed out food, there were kids to be seen that were obviously very poorly taken care of. We in America are so blessed. These children could have been in Somalia,

Afghanistan, England, or the US: they just happened to be in Iraq. We need to give to help these people out. And , that is what we as a Christian nation do. We give.

Printing Money

In 2017, America was functionally broke. Over the previous 10 years, it had put huge amounts of money in creating government jobs to keep individuals employed, but forgot about the small business owners who had helped create the wealth of the country since its inception. Man's government in the US (they had forgotten about God over the last decade), had borrowed money from the Chinese and other governments, and had just printed money with no economic basis or gold backing. In 2017, the value of $1 was the lowest it had ever been. Many individuals who saw this coming, began trading with each other with gold and other valuables.

Mary Thomas was a small business owner from Murphy, Delaware. She understood the trading concept and worked very hard to provide for her family. She took old clothes and scarves and yarn from others who was throwing it away, and she made quilts. She also grew vegetables and fruit in her small yard in Northern Delaware. She no longer had a need for American money. She traded her quilts for milk, meat and materials.

Since the country's inception in 1776, God had given America gold, coal, water, crops, and other commodities; enough to sustain it through each generation. The gold, which still remained under ground in areas throughout America, now lay hidden with no desire to retrieve it.

There were preachers and men who still believed in God who protected America from a final destruction, as Lot tried to protect Sodom and Gomorrah. But, these men were quickly dying, as they were older men with poor health.

As Mary walked to a neighbor's home on a cold, December day, she found a $10 bill floating in the wind. She saw that it no longer said "In God We Trust" but said "America the Beautiful" in its place.

The United States, as a country, so far, has been blessed with little terrorism (except 9/11), a relatively low crime rate, a relatively low unemployment rate (although it is rising), and with opportunities for all. We have a minimum amount of dangerous storms, and a steady logistics system which provides fruits, vegetables, meats, tobacco, and other items to the market on a timely basis at a reasonable price. Who, as an individual, could sit down and design all of the systems that make up the free enterprise system in America and have them work as well as they do? The only one I know is the same being who created man in the first place, along with the heavens and the earth. And, while there is every means to get rich for entrepreneurs and blessed people in America, there are programs in place that benefit middle and low income people also. Look at the system of minimum wage, minimum worker age requirements, the Occupational Health and Safety Act, Social Security, welfare; the list goes on and on. But, America cannot work as a Socialist Country. We need Capitalism because it is what fuels economic growth and tax increase. Lets look at the money cycle of private enterprise versus public enterprise. The private enterprise person (small business owner, corporate worker, etc.) pays taxes from money they individually create by working with private capital. The public worker (government worker, corporation that is dependent on the government for business, etc.) pay taxes off government money (no new taxes are created). Small business creates more new wealth in America each year than anything else. Thus, the focus of government should be to ensure our small businesses succeed, and to create new wealth off assets that God gave us i.e. (Gold, silver, salt, oil).

The make up of America was and is only through the inspiration and blessing of God. And, I am not saying that other countries are not blessed, because they are. However, it is my personal opinion that God has a special place in his heart for America, and blesses it based off how we react to his word and the world. However, here lately, God has gotten to have become just a little sour toward us as a nation. And, with good reason. We openly flaunt homosexuality, which is stated several times throughout the Bible that man shall not be with man, nor for a woman to be with a woman. He also says it is an abomination for a woman to dress like a man. Here recently, President Obama has been supportive of getting rid of "Don't Ask, don't tell in the military." Be openly Gay in today's military? When God clearly speaks against homosexuality in the Bible? I don't even know what an openly Gay person would look like in the military, unless they wore a special uniform that said, look at me, I'm Gay. Why does their sin and downfall have to be brought into my or my children's world? I never discuss with others in the military my sex life with my wife. Why should Gays feel open to discuss their sexual tendencies with me. When they give Gays rights to talk about their sex lives openly, they take away from my rights because I have to give up my religious beliefs to try to accept their way of life. Why is that fair? And, as their are known heterosexual relationships in the military, will we start seeing openly gay relationships in the military? Sick.

But, that is our society. Our largest sin as American's is that we have to look, and by looking, we want to become.   Victoria Secrets has built an empire of stores on that simple downfall of man. Muslim culture cover their women, to protect men from seeing enough of a woman to where there is lust in their heart.   Paul said in the New Testament the same thing, that women should cover their heads, especially when they pray. Women, if they would cover up more, would help decrease sin in America. You've never seen a statistic on that, have you? Just a thought. I know the liberal female would say, why do I have to do this? It is not for you silly. It is because you are doing unto others as you would have them do unto you.   Do you like people making you sin? Unfortunately, the answer to that for 50% of Americans is "who cares." Well, when California falls off into the ocean, you will care. Some began to care more after Hurricane Katrina. Others yet will be moved by the Oil Spill.   You will see things in your life time that generations before you have not seen. Read the King James Version of the Old Testament again for the first time. Things are happening that scientists will relate to previous times, but to God all things are new.

In America, we are helped to sin by giant billboard signs of beautiful women in their underwear advertising the necessity of breast implants. And, there is nothing like watching television with your 11 year old daughter as an old man selling the benefits of Viagra washes through the airwaves. We are riding a wave faster toward destruction than Sodom and Gomorra did, or any society previous to ours. If you ask most college professors, they will say the liberalization of America is for the best, and teach such. In Montana, their is a school system that wants to teach 1st Graders about sex. There is seemingly no way to stop our internal destruction unless we become unified, that we have to do the right things. It is not enough to be a moral leader in this nation, when the people have turned their back and ideals on God. Do you remember how fast Nazi Germany went from a Christian nation to one that believed they were killing millions of Jews for the right reasons? It can happen through sin. One sin, leads to another and another. One lie, leads to another lie and another lie to cover it up. Soon, we have Hitler in office and it is alright to kill large majorities of citizens because of their religious affiliation or non-affiliation?? As your mind says, this could never happen in America........

In Genesis, Chapter 11, God speaks of how the whole world was of one language and of one speech. And they made bricks and they said "go to let us build us a city and a tower whose top may reach unto heaven and let us make us a name. Lest we shall be scattered abroad amongst the surface of the whole earth." And the Lord said "behold the people is one, and they have all one language, and this they begin to do: and now nothing will be restrained from them which they have imagined to do." So the Lord scattered them abroad from them upon the face of all the earth, and they left off to build the city. Therefore the name of it is called Babel, because the Lord did there confound the language of all the earth and from there did the Lord scatter them abroad upon the face of the earth. We, today, through modern technology, media and lack of understanding, have put back together what God once deemed as threatening to him and his will. In Iraq, which I have been privileged enough to do two tours with the military, the world is coming back together. Kellogg-Brown –Root (KBR) hires contractors from all over the world to perform different jobs on US military bases. For example, on one FOB I lived on during my first deployment, the Ukrainians emptied all the "shitters" as we called the porta johns, and disposed of the waste and cleaned them out daily. During my second deployment, the Ugandans guarded the gates, the Russians helped run the flight pad for KBR at FOB Liberty, citizens from India did laundry, and individuals from all over middle eastern countries helped with intelligence gathering. And, recently when the company EODT decided to lower the pay of the Ugandans who were guarding Forward Operating Base (FOB) Stryker and Liberty, near Baghdad, the Ugandans went on strike. This was very Western like. And, in Baghdad, we are on the edge of where God bound the 4 angels in the Euphrates River for 1000 years. We are on the land where God destroyed Babylon, once one of the most powerful cities in the world. And we are bringing back all races of people to this land for the first time since he sent them all away.

Very few people would listen to the words that we are threatening to God, but it may be true. You see, we were separated for a reason. God wants us to know some things, and not to know others. If you see the story of Adam and Eve, God gave them fruit and vegetables and fish to eat in abundance. But, he told them "don't eat from the tree of good and evil." There was a reason. He wanted us not to be caught up in evil. When Eve succumbed to Satan's urging to "just do it," she began the life long downward spiral of sin that has surrounded us for thousands of years. God is there. He wants to protect us. But we have to keep him in our lives.

Sin has always been there. But, here lately, we have been playing even more boldly with things maybe we should not go into. For example, man has been cloning sheep openly, but have they cloned humans behind closed doors? The other day they had a donkey mixed with a Zebra. Was this man made or God made? Man has been doing Embryonic Research, but are they reproducing Embryo's as well. Man is showing ways to change weather patterns, but have they created their own weather as well? We make seeds that are hybrids . We have gone to the moon, and have shot a missile at the moon, to see if we could find water. We have spliced atoms. We have sent cameras to Mars. We have satellites that are around the world, and can see any part of the world within minutes. However, we, with our intelligence and learning, can never defeat God's will. We are destroying our own country and possibly our world, because we are turning our back on what is Biblically right, and going toward what many believe is humanly a right because they don't look at the Bible and have understanding of God's word. No one wants to talk about morality anymore, or doing the right thing. In fact, two of the taboo subjects are religion and politics. To survive, and prosper, we must always keep the fear of God in all that we do and say as a country and as individuals. The Bible teaches us in Proverbs , Chapter 15, vs. 32 "He that refuseth instruction despiseth his own soul; but he that heareth reproof getteth understanding. The fear of the Lord is the instruction of wisdom; and before honor is humility."

In Proverbs, Chapter 22, Vs. 4 it states, "by humility and the fear of the Lord are riches, and honor, and life."

. Have you ever been to a funeral, looked around, seen all of the family present, and asked yourself, "why don't we get together more often." At a funeral, usually a family will put aside petty differences and remember the deceased. Death brings us together. Right now, we as a nation are split between what is morally and ethically right, those who follow Christ, and those who are scientists, who believe that what man creates and deems right is right. Jesus said it best when he said you are either with me, or against me. The time will come when we as a nation will have to make a decision to stand up for the rights that George Washington and Benjamin Franklin and others stood up for. Christians have a right to freedom of religion. Christians also have a right to have their rights defended. This nation was founded on Christianity. Our money says "In God We Trust." Our pledge of allegiance uses the words "one nation, under God." In fact, after the Civil War, it was almost voted in that this nation cannot survive except for the grace of Jesus be added to the Constitution. And, they were right. But, the mass of people will not come together on this until we have the funeral. When thousands upon thousands of people die from losing God's blessing, suddenly the world will wake up. It may take death to get Americans, as well as others, to change their evil ways. It is such a shame.

I write this book not because I am better than anyone else. I write this book not because I know or have visions, or have seen. I write this book because I have lived since 1967 in a world that economically gets better, but morally gets worse, and I love America and see it heading for destruction like the Roman Empire. Because wrong in many cases has become right, and right has become wrong. And, because I am a sinner, whose thoughts and actions rarely reflect that of the sanctity of Christ, but yet that has a relationship with God because Christ Lives. And I know the only way for salvation for myself, my wife, or my children will be through my knowledge and belief in him. It is my prayer that you are moved or touched by something in this book that may help to bring us all closer together as Christians and as true Americans.

America

Have you ever wondered why America is able to have such a strong Democracy when other countries fail at it. Have you ever wondered why we are able to have such an abundance of crops and clean water, while other countries fail at it. Have you ever wondered why our older citizens, for the most part, are able to retire and live in reasonable security until their life passes. Have you ever wondered why we have such serene security throughout our nation, for the most part, contrary to other parts of the world?

The answer could be that we are just lucky. But, ask a bookie in Las Vegas for the odds on a country being able to be as stable as we are, and I bet you will discover that the odds are pretty stacked against it. In fact, we sell at local hardware stores, Wal-Marts, and other sporting goods stores and gun shops the means to create an insurrection or all out war in America; but yet it does not happen. In fact, by the internet, if you wanted to, you could get the ingredients to make different types of explosives, capable to causing catastrophic damage. Google has the answer to everything. Overall, the United States Government gives people the freedom to choose, and for the most part, citizens repay that with doing the right thing.

And, when a citizen chooses to hurt America, as in the Oklahoma bombings, God is the watchful eye. How did Timothy McVeigh get caught? Not through some in depth thought process of analysis of who did what, but through a local police officer doing his job, and thinking or being prodded, "that does not look right." This is how most crime is solved in America and in the world. God puts the right people in the right places at the right time, kind of like little birdies. That which is done in darkness will be brought to the light. As the doubter questions, know that I know there are unsolved crimes according to man. But, no crime has ever been committed throughout the world that God has not been aware of . And, even though the court may not convict all criminals, man has a conscience that is often unforgiving of a lack of judgment. On my second deployment, our Brigade had a convoy out looking at a weapons site that may have had information on Al Qaeda. During the movement, one of the 1151s (an up armored HMMVEE), rode over a pressure plate which set off 2 x 155mm rounds which blew up the HMMVEE and 4 soldiers in it. It took a little time and investigation, but the individuals who were responsible for this were caught. For what man may or may not see, God sees. And, his punishment comes at a time when it is least expected, and upon those who think they are above punishment. Even in the case of a man named Sayf Sabriah (patient sword in Arabic), whose real name was something else. His justice will be served.

We as a country give tremendous aid to other countries, as well as to our own citizens. And, we are obligated to do so. In America, the rights of the poor are protected just like the rights of the wealthy. Several items in the Bible tell us why this is important. Luke 6, Chapter 38 States "Give, and it shall be given unto you, good measure, pressed down and shaken together, and running over, men shall give into your bosom. For with the same measure that you mete withal it shall be measured to you again." We give as a country, because we as a country and sound government understand that the only way to receive is through giving. America gives, and gives, and actually in many cases borrows to give. We understand that peace in our land is through peace and prosperity for all. And, while I am against Civilian Affairs being done by Army soldiers and not by civilians, I can see where the work needs to be done. We are helping poor Iraqis and others have water and food and a chance at a honest government, because it is what God would have us to do. And, the military I guess has to do this because they at least can protect themselves somewhat as they go out and help these people, against powers and principalities that would have them kept in the dark, for their own unfounded beliefs.

It is often said that our government is leading the way toward us becoming a non-Christian nation. As a civilian Police Officer (which I work as a full time job), I will be the first to tell you that I have rarely ever seen a non-Christian Police Officer. Oh, they are out there, including homosexuals and just non-believers. But, they are rarely functional, and rarely last long. And, as a military officer in the Army reserves, I have rarely been to many staff meetings and plans meetings in Iraq or elsewhere to where the first words spoken were that of a Chaplains. In fact, as one questions the depth and gravity of Christ in our Nation, look at the front of most government buildings, and you will see an unfinished stone that is oddly out of place. The unsaid meaning of that stone is from both Psalms 118:22 and Matthew 21:42, as well as other places in the Bible, where Jesus states " the stone which the builders rejected, the same has become the head of the corner: this is the Lords doing, and it is marvelous in our eyes." Do you think it just chance this unfinished stone is at the head of school buildings and government buildings?

Or that perhaps at least a group of men and women have not forgotten our roots.

You see, the soundness and security of what America has, and is, is not from Gross National Product, from the strength of our armed forces, from the intelligence community and their work of gaining knowledge and understanding, or from a 40mm round in a Glock Pistol. The soundness and security of our great nation, the United States of America is from the group of older women and men who attend church every Sunday, who pray for the government, their families, and the needs of those around them, and who give money, food, shelter, and time to those in need and consistently become closer to Christ in their lives. You want to build a good country, help those in the church who are doing the Lords work. You want to build a great county: teach the children to be Christ like in words and deeds, and this next generation will not be worrying about how to stay ahead of the nuclear holocaust, but about what to wear to Church on Sunday, if they cleaned their room well enough, or about making better grades.

The largest item against this change will be Hollywood. You see, as much as human beings have the ability to do good, and to do that which is right, we can't help but look. In fact, our largest sin as humans is that we have to look. Victoria Secrets has built an empire of stores on that simple downfall of man. Muslim culture cover their women, to protect men from seeing enough of a woman to where there is lust in their heart. Muslims still sin, and have to ask forgiveness themselves. The body is at war against the soul.   And, it has always been like this. God gave Lot Angels, who told him to flee Sodom and Gomorrah, because he was going to destroy it, but he told him "look not behind thee, neither stay thou in the plain.." Lot understood, listened, and followed. However, his wife did not listen, turned around and looked, and she became a pillar of salt. You see, the more sensational it is, the more sexy, the more extravagant; the more Hollywood knows you will look. Even if it is against the will of God for you to do so. So, how can we fix it? My approach would be to boycott any movies made in Hollywood until they learn how to make films which have good moral values and decency. But, that would not sell. How do we change this voyeuristic society that we have become?   We, as human beings, cannot change ourselves. However, through prayer and setting this sin before God and asking for help, we could come up with a way to overcome our sin of voyeurism.

Often, people understand that they need to change. For example, I know that the can of skoal I occasionally dip says that it says that it may cause gum disease, mouth cancer, tooth loss, etc. But, I still occasionally dip it because I for some odd and disturbed reason enjoy it. The smoker knows that the cigarettes he or she smokes may cause lung cancer, but they still smoke. In fact, most smokers know someone else who smokes who has cancer, or who has even died from smoking,   but they still smoke because that is not them. That is called apathy. People are for the most part apathetic until it hits them directly. Remember what we talked about with how many families stay apart until one of them dies. Sometimes it takes death to bring us all together.

But, what about the person who has lung cancer. Most, but not all, suddenly become aware that the warnings are to them. They are personally effected by something that is caused by smoking. Suddenly, they want to quit smoking. Most, but not all, can then quit smoking and if healed, go on through life without smoking. Others just say, "well, I am going to die anyway. What does it matter," and keep smoking. I had a next door neighbor who lived beside me when I was growing up who had cancer and he actually I believed started smoking more cigars than he did before he had cancer.

As Jesus said, some of the seeds will go in the soil and plants will come, and other seeds will be just wasted on the soil. The warning I am giving is to all of us, but not all will listen. Part of you will heed the warning, and part will laugh like the kid on Bart Simpson who says "ah ha."

God, knows and understands that we as a world are the same way (apathetic). The Bible is there as a guide. As we read and know that what we are doing is wrong, we shrug our shoulders and say, "well, I know I should not but God will forgive me." For example, lets look at the governor of South Carolina, and his mistress. He used taxpayer money to go to another country to have an affair. He had a beautiful wife, children, and was the governor of the state of South Carolina. He believed it was alright to have an affair because he was the governor. It was a sin. He was proud. He did not repent, and even today has not truly repented I believe. And, he will keep going through life until he does blinded by this pride. One of the things God hates more than anything is pride and insolence. We as a nation have to be smart enough to quit sinning, before we are destroyed. We need to humble ourselves, and understand this path we are on is one that will do nothing but lead to our destruction. But, how do we all get motivated to live right before we, as in the case of our nation, are destroyed completely. Through man, nothing is possible but through God all things are possible.

The best way we as a nation can come together is to embrace our Christian heritage, to accept our evil past, to ask and receive forgiveness, and to learn to do right. We need to teach our children moral values, our adults how to be parents, our leaders how to seek Christ, and all citizens on how to live right. Our political elections should be more on who will seek advice from Christian leaders and God, than from their ability to speak. Our financial markets, banks, and lending institutions should place honesty, as the number one trait they require in new employees. And, they should immediately get rid of the unethical stock brokers, bond traders, government employees, and others who have problems with the truth. We in every way need to learn how to do the right thing. We need to learn to help our neighbor, and to give like we have never given. And we need to pray, that God will turn our hearts from evil, that we may not have to suffer grief. And, we need to pray for those who do not have our beliefs, for them, and their salvation. And, we need to get rid of corruption in every facet of our

lives; in our government, in our businesses, and in
our churches.

The Laws

If I were under the covenant of the Old
Testament, I would have died most likely from
stoning before I was 10. I placed other Gods
(friends, fishing, hunting, working, sports, television,
etc.) before the Lord our God. I cursed, I did not
pay attention in church on Sunday. I did not always
listen to my parents. I took money from my
grandfathers change purse without asking. I lied,
and I wanted things others had. In other words,
from the Old Testament Law, I should have been
stoned early. In fact, by the time I was 14 , you
could add adultery in that as I was chasing every
young girl that might have been interested, with lust
in my eyes. So, I should really not be here writing
this now by biblical standards.

However, I am. And I have been forgiven.
Because God forgives. The blood of Jesus washes
away my sins. It is that simple. God put Jesus on this
earth for one reason: the atonement of our sins.
That those who believe in him as the Christ, will be
forgiven of their sins. It is that simple. He was the
sacrifice that took the place of all the animal
sacrifices in the Old Testament. The scars remain,
but there is new life after being saved.

Many preachers today preach that it does not
matter what you do after you are saved, as you are
saved through the grace of Jesus and that overrides
everything. However, one thing that has not
changed since Jesus has been here, is our soul. You

see, our soul is saved without animal sacrifice any more because Jesus was our salvation. But, we still need to be able to pray to God in our lives. And, sin comes between us and God. Sin is like plaque building up on your teeth. When you get your teeth cleaned, they are pretty and white. When you go several days without brushing your teeth, the teeth turn a dull, yellow look from plaque. The teeth underneath may still be white and healthy, but they cannot be seen for the plaque. The same is the way God sees us when we sin. He cannot see through the plaque on your soul when you sin against him. And, you can tell when he does not hear your prayers. Some people sin so much to where they cannot communicate with God at all. Stopping, starting all over, asking for Gods forgiveness, and fasting will clean the soul again to where God can be involved. I know I can tell a difference when I have unconfessed sin in my life, as I have unanswered prayer. I can tell the difference between when God hears my prayer and doesn't think it's a good idea and when he just doesn't hear. Clean the plaque off your soul, so God can more clearly see and hear you. You may say, what builds the plaque to where God cannot hear your prayers? Not forgiving others, lust, envy, greed, lying, coveting, adultery; the list as you know goes on. Read the King James Bible and pray so you can learn to live without sin in you life. And, believe on your own as you are led.

Jesus in the New Testament changed several laws from the Old Testament. When asked why his disciples took ears of corn off a stalk on the Sabbath, he said basically that if someone was hungry on the Sabbath, they should get corn or whatever and eat.

Or if their donkey went in a ditch, get it out. This directly contradicted the Old Testament teachings. Remember when Moses was told that someone was out picking up Manna on the Sabbath; he had him killed. Jesus came to give us life more abundantly.

And, this freedom was actually forecasted by the Prophet Isaiah. Isaiah said in Chapter 1, verse 10-20: "Hear the word of the Lord ye rulers of Sodom; give ear unto the law of our God, ye people of Gomorrah. To what purpose is the multitude of your sacrifices unto me? Saith the Lord. I am full of the burnt offerings of rams and the fat of fed beasts, and I delight not in the blood of bullocks, or of lambs or of he goats. When you come to appear before me, who hath required this at your hand to tread my courts. Bring no more vain oblation; incense is an abomination to me. The new moons and Sabbaths, the calling of assemblies, I cannot away with. It is iniquity, even the solemn meeting. Your new moons and your appointed feasts, my soul hateth. They are a trouble unto me. I am weary to bear them. And, when you spread forth your hands I will hide mine eyes from you, yea when ye make many prayers, I will not hear, your hands are full of blood. Wash you, make you clean. Put away the evil of your doings from before my eyes, cease to do evil. Learn to do well. Seek judgment, relieve the oppressed, judge the fatherless, plead for the widow. Come now and let us reason together, saith the Lord. Though your sins be as scarlet, they shall be as white as snow. Though they be red like crimson, they shall be as wool. If ye be willing and obedient, ye shall eat the good of the land. But, if ye refuse and rebel, ye shall be devoured with the sword, for the mouth of the Lord hath spoken it."

In Proverbs Chapter 19, vs. 23 it states, "the fear of the Lord tendeth to Life, and he that hath it shall abide satisfied: he shall not be visited by evil."

You can't walk before you can crawl. So lets do a review of some basic rules that God had for his people, which are still applicable today. You see, you can't get where you want to go if you don't know where you are going. And where I want you to go, is to heaven and to have a more abundant life here on earth. And, I want America to survive. And, I want you to see that to live a good life, you have to be honest and true to yourself and others. To do these, you have to fully understand the Bible. Many Christian Churches today preach only on the New Testament. They forget about the Old Testament, and state that was so prehistoric. In fact, they hide parts of the New Testament, like where Paul said women should be covered when they pray, and that women should be quiet in the Church. Very few Churches teach straight out of the Bible today because they are afraid of offending someone.

God clearly taught us how to live in the Old Testament. And, if you believe in Jesus, then you believe in God. If you believe in God, then whether you know it or not, you believe in Jesus. Because Jesus was the son of God. When Jesus prayed, he prayed to his father (God). When we pray, we should pray to his Father also, as he taught us in the Lords Prayer: Our Father, who art in heaven, hallowed be thy name, thy kingdom come, thy will be done, on the earth as it is in heaven, give us this day, our daily bread, and forgive us our trespasses as we forgive those who trespass against us, and lead us not into temptation, but deliver us from evil, for thine is the kingdom, the power and the glory forever. Selah.

God gave laws by presenting the 10 Commandments to Moses. At the time, the people, the beginnings of Israel, were evil. In the time it took for Moses to leave and go get the 10 Commandments and return, the people had already turned toward idols and made of all things an idol to worship. People, from their inner sense, when without Christian leadership, turn to false idols. It is inevitable.

Anyway, when Moses returned to see his corrupt people, the beginning of the Israelis, these were the main laws that he gave them:

Thou shalt have no other Gods before me.

It will Wait

Julie was a fine young girl. She always went to church with her mother and father, and gave her tithes, and read her Bible and said her prayers. She completely understood that God the Father had created the world and all that was in it, and that the only way she was saved for eternity was through her faith in Christ, as she was born a sinner.

Julie had a friend named Allison, that she grew up with and remained friends with even when they were both getting ready to graduate from high school. Julie went to Church sometimes, and was taught about God and Jesus, and knew some of the Bible, but she said she was just not into that . She often made the comment that "yeah, Jesus may be true, but I won't know till I am dead will I."

On a beautiful day, during which people were thinking about being outside and the upcoming weekend, something happened that shocked the world. Julie, her parents, and others who were devoted Christians disappeared from earth. They went to heaven to live an eternity with Jesus.

Allison, and most of her friends, (most others), remained on earth trying to figure out what happened. Many scientists were on television describing how certain molecular events had transpired over the last 24 hours, causing people from all over the world to suddenly disappear. The new world leader was on television telling everyone it was alright, that everyone was alright and to go back to life. In fact, in one large city, they were having a large "its alright " festival with free beer and wine. Allison looked forward to going to it with her friends.......

In American society today, we have become the brain children of putting everything before God. Just like the people Moses led from Egypt, people quickly worship other Gods in the lack of Godly leadership. If you watch the news long enough, we have become accustomed to seeing preachers who are accused of having sex with young boys and girls, and sin abounds. While I was being mobilized to deploy to Iraq my second time, we spent time training at Camp Shelby (near Hattiesburg), Mississippi. While there, I had a chance to listen to a Catholic Priest speak who used the term "Rats Ass," probably 25 times during the 2-3 hours he was speaking. And, no matter what he said, he believed he was right. He spoke as if the Bible was a thing of the past, and his knowledge he learned from other men was that which was right. Charlie Daniels once said, "you know what is wrong with the world today, people done gone put their Bibles away, they are living by the laws of the jungle, not the laws of the land. The good book says, and I know it's the truth, an eye for an eye, and a tooth for a tooth...." We, men , have become so right in our own eyes because man says it is right. Sunday, what used to be in America a day of rest, has become a day of sports. One of the largest lobbying efforts in Raleigh, NC today is to allow hunting on Sundays. What about a lobbying effort in Raleigh, NC to make our children more honest? How about teaching ethics in college? How about having Sunday School as part of the curriculum in Kindergarten? In many cases, men had often rather be seen at a golf course on Sunday morning than at Church. Sporting events, such as Nascar and the National Football League, bring people to their arenas and away from church and family. I have to say though, that during the 600 (Nascar Race) this year at the Lowes Motor Speedway, that Franklin Graham was allowed to talk and pray before the race. (The race was rained out this year on Sunday and had to be run on Monday). I was impressed by this. Perhaps, even race track owners, understand in some small way that there has to be a way for man and God to reach in the middle. If they would just start having major sporting events on Saturday, it would alleviate a lot of the need to "go do something" instead of spending time with God and family "just being."

I don't think men intentionally put other God's before God in most cases, but they do unintentionally because they are not aware. And, it is getting worse because the schools are no longer teaching from the Bible. I believe the United States Government put "In God We Trust" on the American currency because we were given wealth from God, and men would likely store money and place this store of money before God. You know, God gave us oil, gold, silver, corn, wheat, barley, cattle, fish; they were free gifts from God, that man has made a living off of since the beginning of time. As men, we

need to stand up for our families in not putting any Gods before the Lord our God, so that our land may be blessed, and our families may be blessed. In Jeremiah 3, Verses 20-25 the Lord spoke "Surely as a wife treacherously departeth from her husband, so have ye dealt treacherously with me, O house of Israel, saith the Lord. A voice was heard upon the high places weeping and supplications of the children of Israel: for they have perverted their way, and they have forgotten the Lord their God. Return, ye backsliding children, and I will heal your backslidings. Behold, we come into thee. For thou art the Lord our God. Truly in vain is salvation hoped for from the hills, and from the multitude of mountains. Truly in the Lord our God is the salvation of Israel. For shame hath devoured the labor of our fathers from our youth, their flocks and their herds, their sons and their daughters. We lie down in our shame, and our confusion covereth us. For we have sinned against the Lord our God, we and our fathers, from our youth even unto this day, and have not obeyed the voice of the Lord our God. It continues in Chapter 4, "If thou wilt return, O Israel, saith the Lord, return unto me , and if thou wilt put away thine abominations out of my sight, then shalt thou not remove. And thou shalt swear, the Lord liveth, in truth , in judgement, and in righteousness, and the nations shall bless themselves in him, and in him shall they glory."

Thou shalt not make unto thee any graven image, or any likeness of any thing that is in heaven above, or that is in the earth beneath, or that is in the water beneath the earth. Thou shalt not bow down thyself to them, nor serve them, for I the Lord thy God am a jealous God, visiting the iniquity of the fathers upon the children unto the third and fourth generation of them that hate me. And showing mercy to thousands of them that love me and keep my commandments.

The Greeks were bad about this. They would pray to their God's Athena or Zeus, or who ever, and they would make statues of what they believe they looked like. Even today there are sun worshippers and moon worshippers, and for what?   God created the heaven and the earth, the sea, the heavens and all that are therein. There are none of these that represent him. In fact, if you wanted to see the closest thing that images God, look at yourself. Man was created in God's image, in the image of God, created he them. God is omnipresent, but not to be created in any image.

I used to work for a bank based out of Pennsylvania. I travelled one day to the office of a mortgage broker, who worked in an office in downtown Charlotte. The individual who owned the office was of Indian (the country) decent. He had taped up on his wall probably 2000 one-dollar bills. It was like he thought if he had enough of them taped on the wall, he would be blessed. Man made dollar bills. How can you worship money and think that a man/machine made item would return something?

In Isaiah, Chapter 40, the following words are spoken, "To whom then will you liken to God? Or what likeness will ye compare unto him?   The workman melteth a graven image, and the goldsmith spreadeth it over with gold, and casteth silver chains. He that is so impoverished that he hath no oblation chooseth a tree that will not rot; he seeketh unto him a graven image, that shall not be moved. Have ye not known? Have ye not heard? Hath it not been told ye from the beginning? Have ye not understood from the foundations of the earth? It is he that sitteth upon the circle of the earth, and the inhabitants thereof are as grasshoppers; that stretcheth out the heavens as a curtain, and spreadeth them out as a tent to dwell in.   That bringeth the princes to nothing: he maketh the judges of the earth as vanity. Yea, they shall not be planted; yea , they shall not be sown: yea, their stock shall not take root in the earth: and he shall also blow upon them, and they shall shall wither, and the whirlwind shall take them away as stubble. To whom then will ye liken me, or shall I be equal? Saith the Holy One. Lift up your eyes on high, and behold who hath created these things, that bringeth out their host by number: he calleth them all by names by the greatness of his might, for that he is strong in power; not one faileth.

Did you notice that in the verse above that Isaiah said that God sits above the circle of the earth?   Did you know that Isaiah was called into the ministry around 740BC.   Christopher Columbus is often credited for saying the world was round, but even he believed that the world was round because of the work of Isaiah. The secrets, the keys to life,   are in the Bible and in the works and words of God and our savior, Jesus Christ. The world will have you believe that the keys to life are in a conspiracy or complicated government cover up, or that there are no secrets to life. The words are before you in the cover of the Bible, ready for your uncovering as you read and believe.

Thou shalt not take the name of the Lord thy God in vain: for the Lord will not hold him guiltless that taketh his name in vain.

This one makes me cringe. Do not curse God. Things in life are going to happen and you are not going to know why. When bad things happen, people often fall away from God as they are mad with him. God knows what is going on.   Life is long and hard. There is no promise for anyone that they will not see death, financial hard times, health problems, loneliness, failure........these are all things that are in mans life that are going to happen whether you are the largest sinner in the world or walking a very close walk with the Lord. Good things will happen to bad people, and bad things will happen to good people. As Job's wife said when a lot of bad things happened to him, "curse God and die." But, Job did not do that and went on to be restored of everything that was taken from him and more. In the heart of the storm, keep your faith and knowledge in God and know he will pull you through according to his will.

Yesterday, I lost my keys, or better yet my son took them to his grandmother's house. I could not find them. I was late for work. I became very upset. I kept praying for God to show me where my keys were. But, I could not find them in my home, because they were at another house. Finally, when my son got home from school and told me the keys were at his grandmother's house, the answer of where the keys were was solved. I looked to God for an answer. He could not give me that answer because there was someone else involved. I did not use the Lord's name in vain, but I questioned his love. Why could I not just have my keys? Why was that too much to ask? Sometimes, the answers we seek cannot be found except through other people.

For some reason, when some military leaders get upset they take God's name in vain, like suddenly it is going to fix everything. Younger soldiers who see this may think this is the way to act, and then they start saying this. If you are in a position of leadership, then your words and your actions are accountable. You are responsible if you teach a subordinate to sin.

In Ecclesiastes Chapter 3, it is said "To everything thing there is a season, and a time to every purpose under heaven. A time to be born, and a time to die. A time to plant, and a time to pluck up that which is planted. A time to kill, and a time to heal, a time to break down, and a time to build up, a time to weep, and a time to laugh, a time to mourn, and a time to dance, A time to cast away stones, and a time to gather stones together, a time to embrace, and a time to refrain from embracing, a time to get , and a time to lose, a time to keep, and a time to cast away, a time to rend, and a time to sew, a time to keep silence, and a time to speak, a time to love, and a time to hate, a time of war, and a time of peace."

God loves you. He gave you life not so it would be perfect, but that you could live the seasons of life as he created them. For if you were never truly sad, how could you ever be truly happy? Time heals all wounds, and having faith in God during the most trying times, is truly the sign of a Christian and a saint.

Remember the Sabbath day to keep it holy. Six days shalt thou labor and do thy work, but the seventh day is the Sabbath of the Lord thy God: in it thou shalt not do any work , thou, nor thy son, nor thy daughter, thy manservant, nor thy maidservant, nor thy cattle, nor thy stranger that is within thy gates.

We as a society have chosen to abandon this commandment in the name of retail business. Wal Mart, K Mart, Food Lion, Sears and other department stores all open on Sunday now so they can increase sales. I believe it sucks, and if I could I would close all retail stores on Sunday. I know, the Catholics have a Sabbath on Saturday. The Islamic religion worships on Friday sundown through Saturday afternoon. But, America is a Protestant country. Sunday has been our day of rest, and is naturally a day of rest. If you walk outside, there is a difference on Sunday morning from Monday – Saturday. Maybe it is in my head, but the birds are happier, and the sky is bluer, it is naturally quieter, and the countryside is more peaceful. Or am I wrong?

There are some people who would have to still get the ox out of the ditch on Sunday though. These include firefighters, police officers, other emergency workers, hospital workers, etc. If you are getting the ox out of the ditch, it is one thing. If you are at war, it is one thing. If you are selling items to people on their way to and from Church, you are wrong. Jesus turned the tables of the money changers over when they were working at the church on the Sabbath.

All I believe is that we should put God first. If Sunday is considered the Lord's day in America, which it is, then lets put God first and close the stores. The stores will increase their sales on other days to make up for it, and employee's children will see their parents consistently one day a week. The children of this generation will benefit the most by us re-instituting "Blue" Laws.

In Exodus, Chapter 31, Verse 12, "And the Lord spoke unto Moses saying, speak thou also unto the children of Israel, saying, verily my Sabbaths ye shall keep: for it is a sign between me and you, throughout you generations; that ye may know that I am the Lord that doth sanctify you. Ye shall keep the Sabbath therefore, for it is holy unto you. Every one that defileth it shall surely be put to death: for whosoever doeth any work in the Sabbath day, he shall surely be put to death. Wherefore the children of Israel shall keep the Sabbath, to observe the Sabbath throughout their generations, for a perpetual covenant. It is a sign between me and the children of Israel for ever: for in six days the Lord made heaven and earth, and on the seventh day he rested, and was refreshed."

I remember growing up that I had a best friend who's father was very successful in the sales of building supplies. He was a very honest and giving man, who worked very hard and had an office in his house. He would not work on Sunday's though. I remember one Sunday coming into his house and his father told me and my friend to be quiet because it was Sunday. He was on the couch with his wife watching a fireplace, with their daughter sleeping in between them. It was so serene. I don't know why I remember it, but it seemed to be the way that God would want us to be on Sunday. Family, which consists of a father, a mother, and children are gifts from God, are not to be taken lightly, and should be enjoyed, especially on Sunday.

Honor thy father and thy mother, that thy days may be long upon the land which the Lord thy God giveth thee.

This can only be taught at an early age and with a belt. Children who are taught early to fear their mother and father, are more likely to stay on the narrow path. Children who are taught early its alright to lie, will next steal, etc. The path of righteousness is straight but narrow. You can't deviate. The path to hell is wide open. You can do anything you want and get to Hell, 24 hours a day, 7 days a week. It never closes. Those who will argue to spare the rod, spoil the child. The prisons are full of spoiled children, who steal from Wal Mart or Sears because they wanted something.

When I was seventeen, I knew it all. When I was thirty with three children, a house payment, and trying to make ends meet, I realized how little I knew. Life is like this. Your parents know more than you think. We should teach our children to better honor their parents. Once again, as our children are being brought up by Hollywood, they are being taught that it is funny to lie to their parents and get away with it; that deceitfulness goes hand in hand with intelligence; that honesty is not always the best policy. And some liberal from the ACLU is saying, well that's alright. We should not fall to that. We are a better society than to let our children get on drugs and steal because we are afraid to tell the ACLU to get lost. I appreciate the ACLU for Freedom of Speech protection, and other Freedom of Rights. But I do not appreciate the ACLU for taking prayer out of school, or the belief in Christ. Children need to know what right looks like, and Christ is the closest thing to right I have ever seen. Perhaps the ACLU has a substitute they could provide?

In Proverbs, Chapter 19, vs. 26, "He that wasteth his father, and chaseth away his mother, is a son that causeth shame, and bringeth reproach. Cease my son to hear the instruction that causeth to err from the words of knowledge." Today, this instruction that causes children to err is primarily from parents who no longer, for what ever reason, know their own children. They become engrossed in work, or find a new boyfriend or girlfriend after a divorce, or just become lazy. They take no interest in their children and then the children have to make up for this lack of attention by other means. The children often make up for it by watching massive amounts of television. Then, they find friends who say they know more than their parents. These same friends are the ones that will introduce children to marijuana, that say, oh, it is only sex. These friends are the ones who spread the joys of smoking cigarettes, drinking alcohol, reading pornography, and skipping school. These childish activities, then lead children into more devious activities that are harder to come back from such as breaking and entering to steal alcohol, committing armed robbery to get a carton of cigarettes or a Playboy magazine. From skipping school, they become entangled with their boyfriend or girlfriend, which soon creates a possible unwanted pregnancy or sexually transmitted disease. From there, a female may choose to have an abortion, which leads to a lifelong depression and anguish from committing murder. Their self esteem is destroyed because the soul has been scarred. The lifelong downward spiral seems like it is an individual choice, but it can be stopped by parents who love their children enough to discipline them from early in youth.

Yes, ask females who have had abortions. The killing of a baby, even an unborn baby of only 3 months in the womb, is known by the mother in their conscious to be murder. Young men who are caught stealing from stores begin a life long journey of being arrested and then released, until such time as they do something so horrible that it creates hard time in prison. Children say, "it won't happen to me." Parents say, "it won't happen to my child." Well, let me tell you a story about someone who it should not have happened to.

My wife and I got married in 1992. At this time, my wife had a friend who came from a very wealthy and prominent family. This friend came to our wedding and had the look like, "why am I here" while she was there. Her grandfather was a very wealthy man, who actually was involved in the battle of Iwo Jima during WWII, and later went on to build a successful business. She drove nice cars and had a flashy ex-husband, and always had the "I am better than you are air." When I was 24, just out of the Marine Corps and College and making $23000 a year, everyone was better than I was, so I accepted it. However, as time went on, you started to see changes. You see, this friend started doing Crack Cocaine. She had a daughter and husband, and the husband was also well known. Soon, she was divorced and a single mother, because the husband lost his job with the travelling minor league baseball team. She had money, as she was from a wealthy family, but she then began doing more Crack Cocaine, became addicted, and started getting arrested. At that time, her family started to cut her off from money because of the drugs. She later went on to do armed robbery. And, she had a beautiful daughter who needed her mother. She wound up stealing her uncles car and selling it for $500 (it was a Land Rover), and then became a prostitute in one of the worst areas of the city, before finally being arrested and sent away for hard time for drugs. However, you know the worst of it. About 10 years after this, while on routine patrol as a Police Officer, I get a call to a store to respond to a report of some kids who had stolen items from the store. As I walked in, I noticed this child. She was with some friends and had stolen of all things some panties and bras. I was very upset, first of all at her, but secondly at myself because I kept asking myself, what if I would have done something different. What if I had adopted her or something like that? But she was the product of a mother who was a bad parent, who created a child who did not know right from wrong. And, guess what , this child was still in the same family of money her mother was in, and probably had more money on her at 14 than I had on me at 40. Sin, for what ever reason, that seems funny today and like it could cause no harm tomorrow, wipes a little away from your soul. It makes a man or woman unable to speak with God.

It makes a man or woman lose sight of right and wrong. We as humans need to know right and wrong. The atheist will say, well we are descendants of animals , or I don't believe. Well, atheist friend of mine, why do humans blush and animals don't? You want to know why, it is because we are innately possessed with a spirit, whether we want to admit it or not, that knows right and wrong. And, this spirit stays with us until we die. When we die, the spirit goes to heaven or hell. If you know Christ and have asked him for forgiveness of your sins, you go to heaven. If you ignore him, and don't believe, you will be like Lazarus, who when he died and went to hell, he was able to see heaven, and asked Abraham for to cool his tongue. Heaven and hell are real.

God is omnipresent. He sees and knows all. Children today are brought up with all the elements of failure, more so than any time in history. If they do not have loving parents at home who care about them and ensure they are on the right path, in the worst case they become involved in gangs, and as a second worst case they become lost being raised by other kids. The "bloods" and "crips" and "Aryan nation" are all American gangs ready to take on children who do not honor their mother and father, or that are abandoned from their parents for what ever reason. Al Qaeda and the Taliban will also take them. It is not easy for kids to grow up in 2009, especially with the television showing them one way to act and their parents and church telling them another way to act. As Jesus said, you cannot serve man and mammon. You learn to hate the one, and love the other, or love the one, and hate the other.

You cannot serve two bosses. As early as possible, parents should throw the television away, or set the channels to just clear and Christian programming or news. I say this but I have a problem with this too. How do we break ourselves of this weakness without God intervening and destroying? I do not know a way. The body is willing, but the mind is weak. I have children living in this world too and I sometimes do not watch good television. For example, I have watched almost every episode of the Soprano's, but I do not watch it with my children. Most of the episodes that I have seen have been while I am overseas. But, the truth is, it is not good for my mind and soul. I have been as large a hypocrite as anyone. However , the last year I have watched less and less television, and when I do it is news or sports. With God's help, I can break the habit of bad television. With God's help, I can possibly even get rid of television completely in my home.

In Proverbs, Chapter 20, vs. 11 it is said, "even a child is known by his doings, whether his work be pure, and whether it be right. The hearing ear and the seeing eye, the Lord hath made even both of them."

In Proverbs, Chapter 23, vs. 12 there is a message for children who will listen, "apply thine heart unto instruction, and thine ears to the words of knowledge." And then it goes on to say to parents who will listen, " withhold not correction from the child: for if thou beatest him with the rod, he shall not die. Thou shalt beat him with the rod, and deliver his soul from hell. My son, if thine heart be wise, my heart shall rejoice, even mine. Yea, my reins shall rejoice, when thy lips speak right things. Let not thine heart envy sinners; but be thou in the fear of the Lord all the day long. For surely there is an end: and thine expectation shall not be cut off. Hear thou, my son and be wise and guide thine heart in the way. Be not among winebibbers; among riotous eaters of flesh. For the drunkard and the glutton shall come to poverty: and drowsiness shall clothe a man with rags. Hearken unto thy father that begat thee, and despise not thy mother when she is old. Buy the truth, and sell it not; also wisdom, and instruction, and understanding. The father of the righteous shall greatly rejoice and he that begetteth a wise child shall have joy of him. Thy father and thy mother shall be glad, and she that bare thee shall rejoice. My son, give me thine heart, and let thine eyes observe my ways. For a whore is a deep ditch; and a strange woman is a narrow pit. She also lieth in wait as for a prey, and increaseth the transgressors among men. Who hath woe: who hath sorrow: who hath contentions: who hath babbling? Who hath wounds without cause? Who hath redness of eyes? They that tarry long at the wine; they that go to seek mixed wine. Look not thou upon the wine when it is red, when it giveth his color in the cup, when it moveth itself aright. At the last, it biteth like a serpent and stingeth like an adder. Thine eyes shall behold strange women, and thine heart shall utter perverse things. Yea, thou shalt be as he that lieth down in the midst of the sea, or as he that lieth upon the top of a mast. They have stricken me, shalt thou say, and I was not sick, they have beaten me and I felt it not, when shall I awake? I will seek it yet again."   Ah, the plight of the man that drinks too much.   This man, was once a child, who was not taught to honor his mother and father. The people who have the most problems later in life are those who are not disciplined to honor their father and mother as children.

Thou shalt not kill.

As a Police Officer, I have seen several murders. One of the murders was where a boyfriend cut the throat of his girlfriend in their single wide mobile home because she was going to leave him. There were two children in the mobile home. Another, was a drug dealer who was eating a steak on his bed with Heinz 57 sauce, when 2 other drug dealers came in a robbed him. He had a camera at the front of his single wide mobile home that showed them coming in. He had a .38 pistol attached inside his shower for this exact situation. He ran to grab his pistol and was shot dead inside his bathroom. All of this happened while his cousin and two nephews sat in the living room watching cartoons. Also, I saw the murder of a many by his gay lover. The "boyfriend" of this guy got upset, and killed him in the kitchen. He laid dead on the floor of the house for two days, and then the boyfriend got the brilliant idea to burn the body. He went and got gasoline, put it all over the house, soaked the dead guy with it, and burned the body in the attempt to get rid of the corpse. When the fire department arrived, they thought they had just a house fire and rushed in to put it out. Imagine their surprise when they saw what was a dead body being burned in the sub-floor of the house, having burned completely through the floor in the house. These are examples of murders; there is no doubt that these suspects are guilty as sin for committing murder.

However, war is a different deal. As an Army Officer, I would kill to protect the rights of America and my fellow soldiers in combat. I have not seen anything in the Bible that says I cannot protect myself if I am being shot at, or if my fellow soldier's life is in danger. I know the argument would be Jesus's statement that if you get hit on one cheek, then turn the other cheek. Or, his statement do unto others as you would have them do unto you. But, in war, there are extraordinary circumstances. If you don't fight, then not only are you letting your own life go, but you are not taking care of your buddy. My buddy would want me to fight for his survival. Jesus went on to say that there is no greater cause than a man lay down his life for another. Furthermore, there is case after case in the Old Testament about killing because you were at war. Look at David and Goliath. If David would have turned the other cheek the other soldiers would have also been killed. In fact, God blesses men at war in the Bible, if they were right. What did they always do to ensure they were right? They prayed before they went into conflict. During one battle, when Moses holds up his hands as praying to God, the Israelites win, and when his arms started to fail, the enemy started to win. Or go to 2 Samuel 22:33 where it states " God is my strength and power; and he maketh my way perfect. He maketh my feet like hinds feet; and setteth me upon my high places. He teacheth my hands to war; so that a bow of steel is broken by my arms." Or, at 2 Chronicles Chapter 6, Verse 33: "Then hear thou from the heavens, even from thy dwelling place, and do according to all that the stranger calleth to thee for; that all people of the earth may know thy name and fear thee, as doth thy people Israel, and may know that this house which I have built is called by thy name. If thy people go out to war against their enemies by the way that thou shalt send them, and they pray unto thee toward this city which thou hast chosen, and the house which I have built for thy name; then hear thou from the heavens their prayer and their supplication, and maintain their cause." Just about every convoy or mission I have ever been on the leaders of the convoy prays before the mission. And, if he does not, we as individuals are praying silently. It is important in war to have God on your side.

But, there is a fine line in killing for the right reasons going to war, and killing for the wrong reasons. If we go to war, we should be right. We should have the leaders of our nation pray, as well as the leaders of the churches. When we went into Iraq, we were right, because Saddam Hussein was evil. For example, he would hang a whole soccer team if they lost. Or, he would knowingly allow one of his sons to beat and torture men, and feed them to their alligators. He had pallets full of US money and many palaces, and the average citizen of Baghdad lived in poverty and had no drinking water.

And, all this was going on in 2002. I will never forget the prayers that was said at our little church outside of a rural farming community, when soldiers went to war.   We must always pray before a conflict, to make the right decision about going into war, because we put our young soldiers into the circumstance that they may have to kill someone for the wrong reasons if we don't. I know George Bush prayed before he made the decision to go into Iraq. It is as Napoleon once said, "The moral is to the physical as 3:1." We can win any war that God is with us, and our young soldiers can clearly see that we are doing it for the right reasons.   We will always have a stalemate or loss if we go to battle for selfish reasons or without God's blessing. So, that is my thoughts from what I have seen in the Bible on war: if you must kill for war, be right in doing so .

There is no other reason besides war to kill. The drug dealer who kills another drug dealer because he is on his territory, has murdered. Or, the husband who gets so mad at his wife to where he kills her, is a murderer. Or the robber, who loses control and kills the store clerk at the convenience store, is a murderer. There is no justification for any of these. If you intentionally and with malice and forethought kill someone, then you should pay the price to both God and man. The difference once again between man and an animal is that a man knows the difference between right and wrong, and blushes because of it.

We, both America and Israel, have the obligation to protect those around us who are weak, who may have been hurt by their government. We may be called upon to go to Somalia or Guinea or many other places as a government to stop injustices that are occurring. We, as the United States of America, and Israel, Gods own people, are one and should know that what we do should be right. These other countries who run around and blow up their sons and daughters in the name of Allah, are wrong. There is no where in the Koran that I know of that it says to blow up somebody else. If they want to impress Allah, the all knowing, the all forgiving, they should learn forgiveness and repentance.

After all, Abraham was one of the first persons in the Bible to receive saving grace for his sins. What the Islamic people do in the name of Jihad is murder innocent women and men. We as American's and Israel, have a God given obligation to fight these people until they can learn the true meaning of the Koran, without mercy. This fight is not murder; this fight is just as it protects our future sons and daughters from being murdered by these infidels.

Thou shalt not commit adultery.

Anything that comes between you and God is not good for your soul. The lust of a woman, or for a man, can cause damage to your relationship with

God. God says it is good that a man and a woman should come together. He condones marriage. But, he does not condone adultery. Adultery is sex before marriage, or anything you do with lust in your heart toward another. If you see another person, and just think about having sex with them, that is lust, and that is adultery.

The Bible says in the Old Testament, Deuteronomy Chapter 22, Verse 22 "If a man be found lying with a woman married to a husband then they shall both of them die, both the man that lay with the woman, and the woman: so shalt thou put away evil from Israel." In the New Testament, Jesus says the following about adultery in Matthew, Chapter 5, Verse 27: "Ye have heard that it was said by them of old time, thou shalt not commit adultery. But, I say unto you, that who soever looketh on a woman to lust after her hath committed adultery with her already in his heart." Furthermore, he says in Matthew Chapter 5, Verse 31: It hath been said that whosoever shall put away his wife, let him give her a writing of divorcement. But I say unto you, that whosoever shall put away his wife, saving for the cause of fornication, causeth her to commit adultery; and who soever shall marry her that is divorced commiteth adultery." However, Jesus was forgiving of an adultress. John Chapter 8: Jesus went unto the mount of Olives. And early in the morning he came again into the temple and all the people came unto him, and he sat down, and taught them. And the scribes and Pharises brought unto him a woman taken in adultery. And when they had set her in the midst they say unto him, Master this woman was taken in adultery, in the very act. Now

Moses in the law commanded us, that such should be stoned: but what sayest thou? This they said tempting him, that they might have to accuse him. But Jesus stooped down, and with his finger wrote on the ground, as though he heard them not. So when they continued asking him he lifted up himself and said unto them, He that is without sin among you let him first cast a stone at her." And, none of them threw a stone. In fact they all left the area except Jesus and the adultress. Jesus told her "go and sin no more."

You really have to work at this today, especially as a man, as there are so many women that dress so provocatively. It can be overcome though by reading the Bible, and when a provocatively dressed woman walks by, don't look. Just look away. That goes for women toward men also. I will admit that as a man I have little knowledge and understanding of the female mind, although I live with 4 women. But, if you are a woman tempted by a man, turn away. The key here is that you keep your soul clear so you can talk to God. If you get plaque on your soul, it is hard for God to break through.

And, like I said, I do not understand the female mind. But, in the Bible it says that a women should cover her head. It is in the Bible. You can argue it, say you are not going to do it, say it is not fair. That is between you and God. If you wear provocative clothes and you cause a man to sin, then don't you think God will hold you accountable for the sin.

Society today is amazing. I don't know how many people watched the movie "Striptease " a few years ago with Demi Moore. Demi Moore played a stripper who stripped to take care of her daughter. She was like not able to get another job, and so this justified it. Anyway, in the movie, there was a politician, Bert Reynolds, who was corrupt and she helped the police catch the bad politician. In the end of the movie, the strippers were the good guys and the politician was the bad guy. Do you not think this has an impact on the younger generation who watches a movie like that? What would be a thought process out of a movie like that. First of all, a female who is about to flunk out of college may begin thinking, well I will just become a stripper. Or a male who watches a movie like that could start thinking, well strippers are just single moms who are trying to make extra money. Movies like that justify sin for righteousness. You take the person who Biblically we should not appreciate because she makes men commit adultery, at least with their minds, and we leave thinking she is good. We take the politician, who is supposed to be the one helping society, and you leave the movie thinking, wow, what a crepe. I bet all politicians are like that. Maybe we should elect strippers as politicians? It has happened before.

Thou shalt not steal.

   Working as a Police Officer for a city, I have seen time and time again the work of God at work against people who steal or rob, and many times have been actually on the winning side. As Napoleon said, "the morale is like 3:1." We did not always win at the time, but we always won in the end, in one way or another. It just goes to show, to win a war, you don't have to win every battle. But, you do need God on your side.

One day, I went to my assembly like always at the Police Station. During the meeting, the Sergeant would give out information on people to look for or cars to look for during the day on patrol. Well, on this day, the Sergeant said "look for a blue Cadillac." As any Police Officer will tell you, when they put out a bolo like that, suddenly every other car is a blue Cadillac. This half went in one ear and out the other I remember as I was trying to write down something he said previously. Well, I am out on patrol on a main road when I see a blue Cadillac roll past me on the right side and make a right hand turn on red without coming to even a close stop. I decide I was going to at least see who this was, so I pulled in behind the Cadillac going East on this road. Before I can run the tag of the Cadillac, he does a quick u turn and starts heading West on this same road. So, I continue to follow him, and as I am waiting for his tag to come back on my computer, while he starts driving fast and erratically. I began to wonder what was going on, and turn on my lights and start following the vehicle. Someone was talking on the radio, and I was like "hey, I am trying to stop a vehicle heading outbound on this road. It is a Blue Cadillac, license tag..." Before I can get this out, the vehicle wrecks into some other vehicles on this road. I am like, "what the hey. " I stop my car, and everyone is pointing down toward a church. I was confused. I finally figured out the man had jumped and ran down behind a church. He was so fast, I had just seen the wreck and he was already behind the church (about 300 yards away). So, I pull down into the church and start running after this guy. I was embarrassed because I could not give good cross streets to the city dispatcher, who was having a hard time figuring out what was happening. I just kept running. I just kept praying, don't let me lose this guy, who was about a 18 year old black male who was out running me, a 40 year old white man with a heavy bullet proof vest on. The male got to a chain link fence with barbed wire over the top, and jumped over it like it was nothing. I was like, "how am I going to do that?"

As I started to climb up the fence, 2 men from somewhere (nowhere better), that were unloading the trunk of their car, run over with a blanket and place it over the barbed wire so I would not get hung up in the barbed wire. They thought of this. I did not ask, and I would not have probably thought of it. I got over the fence and started running again. I had lost sight of him, but I believed he had run back into a subdivision behind this storage facility. I kept running toward the subdivision. As I entered the subdivision, tired and out of breath, from the woods, I saw an older black gentleman driving by with a Toyota, and stopped him by flagging him down and said, "did you see a young black man running?" He said, "yes, get in," and he drove me to where he saw him at and he was just a little further up the road. I told him to stop before he got too close, because I was not sure if the man was armed . I jumped out and ran toward him, and the chase was on again. I saw a cross street and I called out the street. The city dispatcher was glad to know where I was. I kept running, with him outrunning me. He would jump a fence, and I would barely scrape over the top of it. As I got tired and wanted to quit, I came up to a fence that he had climbed over and a woman ran over from no where and let me in. Then, I lost my radio. I had no communication, and was by myself. I kept running. He was back on the road running again now. I ran behind him and he went back into a yard. I chased him back into a yard, and he went over a huge fence. I looked at the fence and was like "no way," but before I could even try to jump over, a rookie police officer slid on the grass beside me like a professional baseball player, reached under the fence, and grabbed the guys ankle and held it. A lady in the yard, showed me a door to the fence and I went through it and arrested the guy. As I look back on this one case, I see Gods work at hand. (1) I did not realize the car was stolen. (2) I did not realize the guy had jumped from the car until the crowd pointed it out to me. (3) I could not outrun him. (4) I could not have jumped over several fences, especially the one with the barbed wire on it that the men laid the blanket on for me, (5) I did not know where I was. (6) I lost him completely. (7) People arrived from no where and helped me to accomplish what I could not do. (8) The youngest and most inexperienced Police Officer on the force slid face first and grabbed his ankle so I could arrest him. You may say, well, you got lucky. Napoleon would say, the morale have a 3:1 odd. Do you really believe this 3:1 odd is just luck?

Another time, I was on a back street off a main Boulevard, with a brand new truck someone had wrecked and run into a ditch. It did no damage to anything but the truck, and when I arrived no one was in the truck   I was wondering if the truck was stolen, as the truck was brand new and just abandoned, wrecked. The truck belonged to a soldier from a military base and the dispatcher tried to call the soldier with no luck. While I was sitting there trying to decide to tow it or leave it in the ditch,   the soldier arrives drunk, down this road that is not very traveled, and says someone took his truck and wrecked it. First of all, I asked him how he knew his truck was there in the ditch. He did not know. I asked who he lent his truck to, and he slurred out I don't know. Well, I knew he was lying but I could not prove it and he had his own tow truck, and I could not prove he was driving it, and I did not see him wreck it, so I had no case. While I finishing this call, I was called about a woman who's purse had been stolen at a laundry facility off a local road. This was about 10 minutes away, so I automatically had in my mind that I probably would not be able to find the suspect, as he would be away faster than I could get there. Also, there was no K9 (dog) working that night. As I drove toward the laundry, I decided to take a back road, as it was faster than going all the way down the main boulevard. As I drove down this road, just like a deer in headlights, a black male (the suspect) froze as he ran across the road in front of me, holding a purse. I wish I had a camera, because he just stopped in the middle of the road in front of me, facing my car, and his eyes were like "oh shit."   I had to laugh; in fact I did laugh. He started to run behind some apartments and I chased him with my car. After about a minute, he got down on his knees, and said "I give up." I placed him under arrest and he started telling me where her purse was. He had taken things out of it over about a block and we had to go and look for all the items. I took him back to where the victim was, and we looked for all the items. He was about a 18 year old black male, who stated he was going in the military the next day. He said he stole because he needed money. We found most of her stuff, but a little of the cash was missing. She was a waitress in a local restaurant, and had some cash that was strewn somewhere on the ground. For some reason, God wanted this man that night caught, perhaps to straighten out his life and give him a chance to do the right thing in the future. God is forgiving, but first one must come to learn to sin no more.

As the Bible says, a man who is caught stealing that is hungry or thirsty, you can almost feel sorry for. But, he will wind up paying 4 times for that by which was taken. Jesus said, ask and it shall be given to you. God will not with hold that by which is good to you. And, you would be surprised at the generosity of people if you ask. Just ask. If someone turns you away and you are hungry, God will know that. Go to the next person and ask for food.

We as a country may get back to the point to where there are some extremely poor families out there who need our help. If you have, you need to share. If you have not, you need to ask. When America was first being founded back in the late 1700's, there were many men who lost everything they had because they bet on land in the expansion of America West. George Washington had to borrow money to go to his own inauguration. North Carolina was made up of poor farmers who could not or would not pay taxes in Virginia. Georgia was inhabited initially by men who were taken out of debtors prisons and given land in Georgia. During the Great Depression, there were masses of unemployed and desperate families. However, when everything else failed, we turned to God. America has a history of having poor people. America also has a history of having people who are willing to give. We as a nation right now are in the largest deficit in dollar amounts since the end of World War II. We need to come together, but groups such as the ACLU and Acorn and other liberal groups do nothing but tear us apart. The churches are the backbone of this country , and the one great seam that holds us together. If you are poor, and need something, don't steal; go to a local church and ask.

Thou shalt not bear false witness against thy neighbor.

The United States Court System has set up a good system of protecting the innocent. First of all, it generally takes two or more witnesses to prosecute someone. Next, it generally takes evidence to tie someone to the crime. Next, there usually has to be a defined motive. And finally, there has to be an actual defined crime committed, before someone can be convicted.

In some countries, primarily Fundamentalist Islamic countries, you can be accused and convicted of something without it even being defined as a crime. This is exactly how Jesus was tried and convicted. You see, Jesus was convicted of blasphemy against God from the same Jewish people who had previously seen him in the church. There was no crime he had committed, besides trying to get people to live their lives as pleasing to God, and to tell the world more about his father. God wants us to be honest with ourselves and with our lives. He wants us to know him, and through him to live a better life on earth, and when we go to heaven. Saying that someone did something when they did not do it, is a sin.

But, when this speaks of bearing false witness against thy neighbor, it also alludes more. It talks of gossip. It alludes to spreading here say. It alludes to talking before you know. Steven Covey once said it best, when he said "seek first to understand, and then to be understood."

10. Thou shalt not covet thy neighbor's house, thou shalt not covet thy neighbor's wife, nor his manservant, nor his ox, nor his ass, nor anything that is thy neighbors.

We, as American's, are guilty of this very often. We see our neighbor get a new car and the next thing we know we are at the car dealership trying to get a new car. We do not use the word covet, but we use the word compete. We as Americans are very competitive. Unfortunate, this competitiveness is usually driven by covetness. This is a sin, as by coveting things, it places plaque between you and God.

I don't think God ever wanted us to do without, or to need something and not to have it. From the very beginning, he gave Adam and Eve fruit to eat and no worries. Then when they sinned, he basically still gave them the tools and land to farm to grow food.

He gave them cattle and meat. There was nothing we have ever lacked. When Moses took the Israelites out of Egypt into the desert for 40 years, God gave them water and manna. They had to ask, but it was given to them.

Look at this great nation we have and the blessings that have been bestowed upon us.

We have a fair set of laws and governance, we usually have a means to make a living, we usually have money in our pockets. If we lack, it is usually in the things we want, and not in the things we truly need.

However, God does not give us everything we want, and we should learn to accept it. Acceptance is one of the keys to happiness. Work hard , pray and do the best you can. And, at the end of the day, know that you did the best you could. Do you remember George Washington having to borrow money to go to the Philadelphia Convention. Do you not think he would have rather God blessed him with the money?   Ask, and it shalt be given to you. When we look at things others have with lust in our hearts, it puts something between us and God. We have to keep our hearts and minds clean in order to effectively communicate with God. It is not easy. Nothing in this world is easy. But doing the hard right thing is so much more important in the long run than taking short cuts.   Be a good neighbor and don't even recognize what your neighbor has. The Arabs call this the evil eye. Did you know that if you go in some homes in an Islamic country, that if you talk about how you like something they feel obligated to give it to you. They would rather give you something than for you to have lust in your heart. I give the Muslims points on their forethought on this. If only they could use such vision in this pointless war against the West.

Also, in Islamic countries, they keep their women covered up. We in America think that this is because they are trying to hold them down, or that they are considered lower than men. In reality, it is because they understand that lust drives sin in a mans heart. If a man sees a woman and has lust for her, he has sinned, which could lead to more sin. If women are covered up, it at least reduces the chance of lust and coveting someone else's wife. We as American's could learn a thing or two from our Islamic brothers, of from Paul   in the Bible. We, as American's and church going folk ourselves, have turned from that which we know is right and made it wrong for Hollywood's sake, as well as to appease to our need to see. We as Americans like to watch.

Jesus's Commandments

After these Commandments, Jesus added two more commandments, or stated that these 2 sum up all the others. These are to Love the Lord your God with all your heart , and with all mind, and with all your soul and to do unto others as you would have them do unto you.

To love the Lord your God with all your heart and all your mind and with all your soul, you have to give up sin. You have to walk on earth with a clean mind and soul. Jesus was one of the only men who ever walked on the earth with a clean mind and soul, and probably will be. You see, Noah, Moses, Job, Isaiah, Jeremiah, David, Solomon, John the Baptist, etc.: they are men in the Bible but their lives were not clean. However , they had a relationship with the Father so great to where God overlooked their human dimensions. Make the fact that you love God part of your daily focus.

To do unto others as you would have them do unto you. This is so easy in words, but so hard in practice, especially in the year 2009. We are in such a hurry. We open and close doors at stores so fast, we don't even see who is coming in behind us. We rush to the front of the line to be served first. We take the last cup of coffee at work and don't make another pot. We go to someone else's house and eat dinner, and don't help to wash the dishes. We let loved ones birthdays go by, and don't even call to wish them a Happy Birthday, or send a card.

According to Proverbs, Chapter 6, Verse 16, "these six things doth the Lord hate, yea, seven are an abomination unto him. A proud look, a lying tongue, and hands that shed innocent blood. A heart that deviseth wicked imaginations, feet that be swift in running to mischief, a false witness that speaketh lies, and he that soweth discord among brothers. "

There are three things we should have to be close to God: (1) the fear of the Lord, and (2) wisdom, and (3) understanding.

The fear of the Lord, according to Proverbs, Chapter 8, verse 13 states that "the fear of the Lord is to hate evil, pride, and arrogancy, and the evil way, and the forward mouth, do I hate."

Wisdom comes from the Lord. In Proverbs, Chapter 2, Verse 6, the Bible says "For the Lord giveth wisdom, out of his mouth cometh knowledge and understanding. He layeth up sound wisdom for the righteous: he is a buckler to them that walk uprightly. He keepeth the paths of judgement, and preserveth the way of his saints. Then shall thou understand righteousness, and judgement, and equity; yea every good path. When wisdom entereth into thine heart, and knowledge is pleasant unto thy soul; discretion shall preserve thee, understanding shall keep thee. To deliver thee from the way of the evil man, from the man that speaketh forward things." Therefore, to obtain wisdom, one should obtain knowledge of the ways of God, by reading the Bible, and practice right conduct, by living what you read.

Understanding also comes from the Lord. One of the most significant parts of the Bible is when Solomon, who could have asked God for anything, asks for understanding. 1 Kings Chapter 8 says "And now, O Lord my God, thou hast made thy servant king instead of David my father; and I am but a little child: I know not how to go out or come in. And thy servant is in the midst of thy people (Israel) which thou hast chosen, a great people, that cannot be numbered nor counted for multitude. Give therefore thy servant an understanding heart to judge thy people, that I may discern between good and bad: for who is able to judge this thy so great a people? And the speech pleased the Lord, that Solomon had asked this thing. And God said unto him, because thou hast asked this thing, and hast not asked for thyself long life, neither hast asked riches for thyself, nor hast asked the life of thine enemies: but hast asked for thyself understanding to discern judgment; behold I have given thee as wise and understanding heart, so that there was none like thee before thee, neither shall any arise like unto thee." Solomon went on to show that he was like none before him, or after him with the ability to discern good and evil.

One last piece of information I will share with you before I go forward. That is how we should pray. Jesus taught us how to pray in the Lords Prayer, as he prayed "Our Father, who art in heaven, hallowed be thy name. Thy kingdom come, thy will be done, on earth as it is in heaven. Give us this day our daily bread, and forgive us our trespasses as we forgive those who trespass against us, and lead us not into temptation, but deliver us from evil, for thou are the kingdom, the power and the glory forever. Amen.

Just pray. Pray for your own wisdom and understanding. Pray for peace for Israel and for our world. Pray for the President of the United States and his family.

Alcohol

When I was about 8, my grandfather, the owner of a skating rink and railroad worker, who worked for a train company for over 50 years, let me have my first taste of beer. This would have been in the mid seventies. He drank Red, White and Blue. I respected my grandfather, because he worked very hard and always had a lot of money. He had a beer mug he would keep in the freezer, and would drink a Red, White , and Blue usually every Saturday night after he closed the Skating Rink. Back then, I could not stand the taste of beer, and would cringe as I tasted it. I always said in my mind, I will never drink this, and I don't know why others would drink it.

When I was in high school,   everyone who was cool and in the "in " crowd went to parties on Friday nights. I remember hearing kids talk about how much fun they had and I envied them. You see my mom made me stay at home, because she had understanding. I was at that time shy, and unsure of myself, as I still am at 42. My father had been out of work after leaving a bank for about a year or so before finding a new job with a Trust Company, and I lived near some very wealthy and blessed families. To hear these kids talk, well, I just wanted to be like everyone else. I used to beg my mother to go out, and she would not let me because she was afraid I would get in trouble. In 1982 I tried out and made the high school football team. I was a Split End, or receiver. It was one of the highlights of my childhood,   and I remember thinking I was someone. One of my best friends back then, that I had grown up with since kindergarten, was going out on a Friday night and I finally talked my mother into letting me go out. I remember that night it was cold, and I was wearing blue jeans and a flannel shirt. We went driving around town in someone's Camaro, I can't remember who's. I remember thinking how nice it was to ride around with friends. While I was in the car, the others could easily carry on conversations about things, but I had trouble fitting in the conversation, much as I have trouble fitting into conversations today. The people in the car stopped and got some beer. I remember drinking one and thinking once again how bad it tasted. But, I drank 2 or 3 Mickeys Wide Mouths, and felt like crap. We finally made it back to school. I wound up drunk and threw up in the front of some bushes at the school. I felt very sick. I decided to try to go to the dance anyway. Someone told the Principal and he made me go to the office, and had my mother picked me up.   She was very upset with me as any parent who was called to school to pick up their intoxicated 15 year old son would be. I was drunk, and had humiliated my mother, and my family. I had to quit the football team. I became depressed, which lasted throughout my high school years and until I went into the Marine Corps. You see, I felt like I was the worst kid in the world. My self esteem did not exist any more. I remember thinking that I was the worst kid in the world. And, this was over one night with a couple of beers. A little harmless fun. In reality, it would have been more fun to have stayed at home and watched the Dukes of Hazard and Dallas. I was upset and depressed. You see, I could not understand why I had to get caught and others did not. I never understood this until years later, that God would have a plan for my life and he did not want alcohol in it.

Move forward a few years until 1999, when my wife was very sick with Multiple Sclerosis, and I had 3 young children of my own at home, and I had a small business I had just started and was not making enough money to pay the bills, and had to take care of both the kids and my wife on top of that stress. I just could not focus with my wife being sick, and the kids, then 2, 4, and 6 needing attention, and everything in my life revolved around being at home to take care of family and nothing seemed to be a blessing at work. I was failing again, and could feel the shame coming on just like high school. I was facing bankruptcy, and with it the loss of my home, my cars, some land I had bought; everything. I remember feeling as if I was hanging off the side of a cliff, and a tiny, frayed piece of string was all that was keeping me from falling. I could and still can see that tiny, frayed piece of string even in my mind today. That tiny, frayed piece of string was my faith back then. I prayed, but I had lost my faith, except for just a little bit. I began drinking. I prayed harder, and nothing happened. I remember how Jim Beam in a glass with ice and orange juice would make me feel better. I would drink one glass, then one more, and sometimes up to half a fifth before I would go to bed. I was not a mean drunk. I was just a drunk who went inside himself. I would check on the kids, and would check on My wife, and even really clean the house really good while I was drinking, with the justification that a little alcohol would not hurt me. In fact, I made it to where I only drank one night a week, on Thursday night. I justified it to myself and to my wife by saying , well, Jesus drank wine. Paul said a little wine for thy infirmities sake. I had every excuse to keep a bottle inside of my desk. I started drinking even more as that ominous day of March, 1999 loomed over me when I had to throw in the towel and file bankruptcy. I was about to lose everything. I went to an attorney in Maxton, NC and filed bankruptcy. I lost everything but my family. The US government took over and sold the land in the mountains. I borrowed $5,000 from my parents to buy 2 used cars, that to this day they have not let me pay back. I was ashamed and did not talk to anyone. I had no friends, and even today have a habit of putting up a wall in my life to where I do not let friends in.

I believed God could work miracles in my life, but I felt he chose not to. My wife was sick all the time, and we had to take her to a lot of different hospitals and medical clinics for treatment. My oldest daughter, who was then 6, was old enough to sense the pain, and was old enough to know what was happening.   I remember hoping and praying that some miracle would happen to where I could afford to pay my house payment and my car payments from arrears and the medical bills. But, it did not happen.   My 6 year old daughter was there, watching. I believe it has had an impact on her even today.

I remember loading up my truck with all of our possessions over a weekend and moving into another home that we rented. It was a big old farm house, that belonged to a farming family since the 1860s. When they plowed outside of it, field mice would run in and freak my wife and the kids out.   I chopped wood and burned it in the fireplace to help keep the drafty house warm, with little avail. We stayed in this house about 3 months, and then moved to a smaller home that I rented and lived there for about 1 year. I got a job with the state. We did not have as much money as we were used to making before I started my business, but we learned to get by. It was sort of like the boy with the fish, when Jesus wanted to feed the masses. I learned that with some faith, even a little goes a long way. During that year (2000), something happened.   I slowly replaced drinking alcohol with reading the

Bible. I was humbled because I was shamed. About the year 2001, I started getting some understanding on what had gone on in my life over the last few years. You know, I made a lot of money off doing mortgages for people from 1994-1999. I charged exorbitant usury on some of these. God said we are not to charge exorbitant usury. I was a proud person during these years, being commissioned an officer in the military in 1993, and buying a Porsche 911 for myself in 1996. I was proud. God cannot stand a proud look.

I never cheated on my wife, probably to no doing of my own, but I had lustful looks when I went out to clubs. I even went out to topless clubs every now and then with friends from work. God said to even look on another with lust in the eyes is the same thing as committing adultery. When I drank alcohol, I never just had 1 or 2 drinks. No matter how well I controlled myself, I was a drunkard. God said that no drunkard would make it into the kingdom of heaven. God wanted me to change. He wanted me to come back to him, and he knew I would not as long as I had everything I wanted. So, he took it all away. He allowed my wife to have Multiple Sclerosis. He allowed me to fail at business. He allowed me to lose everything. Just like Job. Except Job was right with God before he lost everything. I was wrong with God and lost everything. I would often go into bits of uncontrolled crying while I was driving to work, to where I would have to pull off the side of the road.

I came to realize by the end of 2002 that I had been brought low because it was the only way for

God to get my attention. You see, God punishes his children. During the year 2002, for the first time, I read the whole Bible from Genesis to Revelations. Since then, I make a habit to do every year. And, I started to pray every day. At first, when I was beginning to understand God more, I had selfish prayers which came to nothing. As I started to get stronger in my faith and in my relationship with God, I started having stronger prayers. At times, I could tell when prayers went through. If you truly look at the Lords prayer, what does he say: he says a prayer for his will to be done. Our prayers should model this. God wants us to pray for that which is right.

The first year I read through the Bible, I became more and more confused as I finished the Old Testament and then went into the New Testament. It was because I was trying to separate the God of the Old Testament with the God of the New Testament. I could not get that Jesus was not taking God's place, he was just the continuation of God. The second time I read it, I gained more understanding. Each year God gives me more and more understanding. Today, I know that they are all interrelated. I understand that God is God, and there are three parts to him: the father, the son, and the Holy Spirit. I am now 42 years old as I write this. I have only really started to have a good relationship to where I try to walk with him correctly for about 5 years. It takes a lot to get through my head. Others have a strong relationship with God from the beginning.

I slowly have been able to rebuild my life, but God is slow to give me back that he has taken away I think because he knows of my weaknesses of pride, alcohol, and forgetfulness. I completely gave up alcohol in 2003 when I deployed to Iraq for the first time. I say completely, but when I came back from Iraq in 2004, I tried a beer but it tasted nasty, just like it did when I was 8 years old. Even today, as I write this, I am against alcohol, and have not drank. Mainly, it is because of how it existed in my life at two of the lowest periods of my life. But, more than that, it comes between me and the relationship I want to have with God. It dulls and hardens the senses of the temple of God. People of several denominations of churches believe alcohol is alright. But you know, to live a Godly life, you have to always be on the watch. There are billboard signs of women that will make you lust. And we all want to look. There are other temptations in life that are sin, and alcohol just loosens the mind up to say, what the heck. Alcohol, the use of it, may not be a sin. But it clouds the temple (the mind and body) which can cause a man to sin. As you spend time with God in the future, it is my hope and desire that you give up alcohol completely so that your body may become clean to stand before God. Selah.

Miracles

Recently, I was sitting in a worship service with a Army Chaplain, and he spoke on how we should discount miracles and should understand that miraculous things may happen around us, but that we should focus on our faith instead of the miracles. I kept thinking that the miracles were a result of our faith, or at the least, in spite of it. While we should focus on our faith, we should never discount miracles, as they are from God. For God is in charge of all, both good and evil and he works with both to accomplish his will on earth.

Last February (2009), I was at Camp Shelby, Mississippi preparing to go to Iraq with my unit. One of my friends went to a Catholic Church in Hattiesburg, Mississippi, and some how connected with a Priest who was going to Brett Fauves house to watch the super bowl.   Brett invited this Priest to his home, who invited this friend to his house, and ultimately I got to tag along. I think this was one of the neatest things that had ever happened to me, and it was amazing going to his house and watching the game and being within an arms length of one of the greatest football players of all times, Brett Fauve. He was very humble, and I kept thinking how blessed he and his family were, and how he had a great life in Hattiesburg. But, even that night, Brett said he and his wife were praying that he could play again. He wanted to play the next season, but his shoulder was hurt. I remember thinking that it would be a miracle if he could play again, due to his age and the number of years he had played football.

Move ahead to Football Season, 2009. Brett Fauve not only is the starting quarterback for the Minnesota Vikings, but they are now 4-0. Minnesota has all chances of making the Super bowl this year, and Brett is the leader. I know him and his family, from the one short night I was at his home, to be a deeply spiritual persons. And if you watch him on television, you will see how humble he is and how he gives credit to the team, and not to himself. He is very careful to never be too proud. I will probably never see him again through life, but as I watch the season unfold for him this year, I have to believe it to be miraculous, just from the first 4 games. If he loses every game from here on out, he was still blessed from the injury he had last season (2008-2009).

One of the interesting things about his home is that he has built a wall around all of his land, how ever much he has, and inside of this wall is his personal deer. They are able to roam freely in the land within the fence. Mr. Fauve hunts and kills his own deer from his farm. He has also built his mother-in-law a house on their land, and she lives across a lake.

Anyway, miracles happen all the time and we are too eager in 2009 to discount them. We want to believe in luck or fate. But, the truth is God works miracles every day, whether we see them or not. You want to see a miracle, look at the kids that are graduating from high school that have one or both parents deployed overseas with the military. Or look at Lance Armstrong, who survived cancer to go on and win the Tour De France again. Or look at the number of deer that survive every year in urban areas.

My wife, as I said earlier, has Multiple Sclerosis. In 1998, she was told she may not live long because of the scarring on her brain. We were both devastated. We listened to all the doctors. We had young children. She was a special education teacher, and was led to be such. As the disease developed, she would start on one medicine, her body would react to it , and then she would have to switch to a different type of medicine. She took all the medicines that they were recommending, to the point that she overloaded her liver, and started turning a brownish yellow color. She had to quit teaching because she kept passing out at school. We both came to the conclusion by 2001 that if she was going to live, it would be by coming off the medicines and having faith that God would heal her, instead of believing in the medicines. She came off all medicines in 2001. It is now 2009 and she has been relatively healthy except for minor relapses since 2001. She takes only limited medicine now (for her thyroid), and has her skin color back and can drive during the day. To us, this has been a miracle.

But, I have seen miracles throughout my life. I remember when I was 17 and was driving on a road back from work and the road was wet or icy, and I lost control of my 1976 Monte Carlo. I remember that the car went around and around (front to rear) on a road at about 50-70 mph, and I remember thinking this was it. I believe I even went out for a few seconds. When I came to, my car was in a ditch on the side of the road. The car had come to a stop on its on, and had turned off. I sat there for a second and even wondered if I was still alive, or if I was dead and could just see everything. I touched my arm to make sure. I reached down and turned the car ignition on, and it cranked right back up. I pulled up out of the ditch and the car drove just like nothing had happened. I drove home, and looked at the car from the side, and the only damage to the car was some mud on the back bumper, no scratches or anything. This was a miracle.

One evening, when me and My wife had moved into the large white house I spoke of earlier, me and the kids were playing in the kitchen of this house. The house was an old farm house, and it had old glass windows in the kitchen, with like a sun room outside of this kitchen. One of the kids threw a ball, and it knocked a piece of glass out of a window right on top of my daughter's head (who was 2 then). The glass did not break, and it did not even leave a scar on top of my daughters head. Me and my son and my daughter kept looking at my youngest daughter thinking, wow, that was a miracle.

One night, while I was training at Fort Irwin, California prior to my first deployment, I had a call to pick up a German Officer from the Brigade Tactical Operations Center (TOC), and that he would be with us through the deployment. The desert of the National Training Center is very rocky, with steep ravines, and mountainous desert. It is about ½ way between Las Angeles, California and Las Vegas, Nevada. I had a new type of Night Vision Goggles, that were not working very well, PVS-7s I believe, and you were not allowed to turn your lights on during this training. I remember riding up to pick him up, and I was able to see pretty well going down the road because of the light of the moon, and there was a large chemical light on the front of the Brigade TOC. I parked in front. I placed the German Officer in the back of the HMMVV with his gear, and I started going back up the road to where my M577(Command Carrier) was. As I was driving, I felt I was not going right. I kept going, and could barely see the road. As I got to the point I really felt lost, and needed to stop to see if I could figure out where I was, I went over a cliff in the HMMVEE, with the German Officer in the back. I remember thinking, this is it and braced for the worst. Miraculously, the ravine bottomed out in a curved fashion in the bottom and I went back straight about 30 feet down. If it did not curve out, I would have hit head first down the hill and me and the German Officer would have been killed. But, God saw another plan. Even more miraculously, when I looked up after going down the hill, we were at my M577. The German Officer had his arm slightly scraped from the wood on the back of the HMMVEE. He never said anything about it but he had to think I was crazy. He never knew how close we both could have come to dying. God had something more in store for both of us.

Miracles should never be discounted because they are God's way of working in our life. God put you on the earth to accomplish something. As Napoleon said, the moral is to the physical, as 3:1.

As a Police Officer, I have previously told about me chasing the young suspect, who stole the blue Cadillac and I miraculously was able to catch him. If God did not want me to catch him, he was young enough and fast enough to get away from me. But God put two men with a blanket by a fence as I climbed over, a man with a car in my path to take me up to where he had last seen him, and people at their fences to open them for me as I got too tired to jump over. All this, because he wanted me to stop this young man. When you are in the will of God, you are more than likely to see miracles.

One night, an individual who was intoxicated decided to try to outrun a Police Officer down a local road. What just about every one who tries to outrun the police forgets in our town is that this main road ends and you either have to take a right or a left. Well, this young soldier and his buddy, who were driving about a 1985 Ford F150 short bed pick up truck, had no clue the road ended. They went straight through the intersection at about 75 MPH, went airborne, and landed inverted in the truck suspended in the air where they landed in the front of a portable storage building. When I arrived on scene, there were several other officers already there and we all just stared at unbelief. Here were two, young Caucasian males, who had landed inverted in this truck, and the whole roof had been pulled off the truck. They were both being suspended in the air by their seat belts, which kept them in the truck. Their heads were leaning forward from the suspension of the truck. Neither one of them had much bleeding, and they were both coherent but still drunk. The passenger had his shoes and socks torn off his feet, from the impact, but his feet were not scratched. For some reason God wanted these two individuals to live. If you ask anyone about this accident and the position of the two men dangling 20 feet off the ground with the truck inverted and them both able to talk, they would have to tell you it was a miracle. Someone might discount it, but they would have to be awful unbelieving, to the point of trying not to believe.

I have seen a soldier who had a piece of shrapnel hit him 1" from his neck on his bullet proof vest. I have seen a soldier shot by a sniper in the front of his vest. I know of two police officers who were shot in their bullet proof vest and lived. Man created the bullet proof vest. But God made the miracle of man, and blessed his thoughts and actions. "The morale is to the physical as 3:1." Napoleon Bonaparte. If you are questioning whether God has the ability to give us miracles in the 21st century, or at all for that manner, look at your own life. Your life is a miracle, that you can't explain. You cannot explain the life force that runs through your veins, or where that life force goes after you die unless you understand Jesus and the miracle of your life. You have a God given purpose. When you have fulfilled that purpose, and God deems it time, you will travel on. Make the right decision on where you will spend eternity by accepting that God is almighty, and that he sent Jesus to be the Christ that died on the Cross as a final sin payment for mankind's sins. No more animal sacrifices; just Jesus, the Son of God.   And, your acceptance of this simple fact.

Why do I need Jesus

For many years, I was lost. As I said before, during my early years of marriage with my wife, and before that, I saw nothing wrong with drinking, and had looked at pornography like it was a comedy. I had for years sinned, and God had to be fairly upset with my actions. I had even been married before. I got married when I was 19 in a selfish act of trying to cure the loneliness of being a young Marine straight out of boot camp. It was not love: it was lust and loneliness as I look back. And, 2 months after I got married, I got sent to Okinawa, Japan and shortly after that, heard in a phone call from my "wife" that she was seeing someone else and was divorcing me. So, my 1st marriage ended in less than 4 months. Through this action, I not only sinned, but I caused this young lady to sin also. Young people, look at your actions before you rush into marriage, as the exit is always sinful. I am scarred from this. She is scarred from this. Forgiveness of sin is one thing, but the scars do not go away. And, a bad marriage no matter how childish, is a scar that stays with you for life. I am embarrassed to even talk to my kids about it.

Anyway,   when I was stationed on the East Coast, I would drive by a certain university every time I would travel back to base from my parent's house. I would every time see a sign that said the college's name. For some reason, every time I drove by, I felt a tug, sort of like I was supposed to go there. I did not know why. I had planned when I got out of the Marine Corps to go to another college, and start back at what I had started in those years. But, anyway, I kept getting that tug. I applied for and got accepted to both colleges. I started summer school when I got out of the Marine Corps at one school. But, for some reason I kept getting pulled inside to go to the other school. I did not know why. In August, I followed this pull, and with the help of my parents went to this university, and paid tuition and room and board for the Fall Semester. I was not really sure why I was there, but was in the Bachelors of Arts in Economics program, and started. On the very first night I was on campus, I went with my room mate to a Baptist Student Union Meeting. I had no real interest in meeting any one, but you know I met my wife that very first night. She was beautiful, and a real person , and it was not lust, it was like, well we were supposed to be together. You see, that tug that I felt in my soul, which I can barely explain, led me to my wife, and I graduated from this college in the early nineties with a Bachelors Degree in Economics. Me and My wife were married in May the next year. My wife was who I was supposed to spend my life with.

I always will, and always have, regretted rushing into the marriage with my first wife. As I said earlier, it was a sin against God on my part, and it took a lot out of my person. I am ashamed about it, and have barely talked about it since that day. I need Jesus because I am the worst sinner on earth, and my past by Mosaic Law should have had me stoned. But, through the disposition of Jesus, I am forgiven, and I thank him for it.

God forgives, and part of that forgiveness I believe is my wife, and the wonderful four children she has given me, and the life we have built together. I, on the other hand, have had a hard time forgiving myself over this. Others forgave; God forgave; I never forgave myself for years.

Since I was a child, I went to church. I read parts of the Bible that was put in front of me. I would focus on one part or another, but never really get understanding. I have heard several preachers speak on that you really only need the New Testament, and that the Old Testament is not needed. And, for a lot of people, I believe that this is true.

But, I am not that smart. I can't start a math problem in the middle of it and figure it out. I have to start at the beginning and try to figure it out. When I was in college, I could not start learning about Economics in the middle of the book, and have the same understanding that I would have if I began at the beginning of the book. Most soldiers will tell you, Officers who have time as an enlisted soldier have an easier time leading others than those who come straight out of college and start telling people what to do. A lot of it is because an older, experienced soldier shows a person how to do things, where as a younger person tells them what to do.

I have been snow skiing a couple of times. My problem when I went was that I would try to learn to ski by going to the top of the advance course instead of starting at the beginners slope. I did not want to begin by being a beginner. But that is what I was.

It is the same with Christ. We all want to begin our Christian walk believing we are saved; and now we have understanding, and many of us want to immediately run before we crawl. But, as a Christian, we may need to crawl, then walk, then run, and then we may fall back down again, and have to start all over again. That is alright.

You see, it is hard to start anything in life, including life itself, without taking baby steps to learn how to walk. The foundation of a Christian is simple: to Love the Lord your God with all your heart and with all your mind and with all your soul, and to do unto others as you would have them do unto you. And then, to believe that you are a sinner and ask Jesus to forgive you of your sins and to believe that he died on the cross for your sins.

I know that this sounds simple, and it truly is. But, the understanding part is where the Bible comes in. You can be saved through accepting and faith. However, you need the Bible to build a long lasting, close, understanding relationship with God.

The Old Testament gives us the foundation for a good Christian life. You see in it, the pre-cursors to Christ coming. Jesus was predicted by Isaiah, and several other prophets in the Old Testament.

God usually does not start any action without a warning or a pre-cursor. The pre-cursor to Jesus was when God requested of Abraham to take his beloved son, Isaac, to the land of Mariah, and sacrifice him as a burnt offering to him for sin. The Bible never even says that Abraham questions this. He just gets up the next morning, saddles his ass, and takes his son to Moriah. On top of the mountain, his son says " behold the fire and the wood, but where is the lamb for the burnt offering," to which Abraham replies to him, "my son, God will provide himself a lamb for a burnt offering." In Genesis Chapter 21, Verse 9 "And they came to the place which God had told him of, and Abraham built an altar there and laid the wood in order, and bound Isaac his son, and laid him on the altar upon the wood. And Abraham stretched forth his hand, and took the knife to slay his son. And the angel of the Lord called unto him out of heaven , and said, Abraham, Abraham: and he said , here am I. And he said, Lay not thine hand upon the lad neither do thou anything to him: for now I know that thou fearest God, seeing that thou hast not withheld thy son, thine only son from me. And Abraham lifted up his eyes, and looked, and behold behind him a ram caught in a thicket by his horns, and Abraham went and took the ran and offered him up for a burnt offering in the stead of his son. And Abraham called the name of that place, Jehovah-jireh, as it is called to this day. In the mount of the Lord it shall be seen."

You see, God required in the early mosaic times a sacrifice to be slaughtered and killed and burnt on an altar as a sin offering. Early in Moses times, it was done by the individuals themselves. Later on, it became slaughtered and killed by the priest, as only the correct individuals were worthy to offer the sin offering.

Jesus came and took all of this away. When Jesus was sacrificed on the cross, an individual, such as you and me, can accept him as our sacrifice, and our sins are forgiven us. Now, I read the Bible every year, and I understand from what it says how it works, but it is difficult to comprehend unless you just accept. Jesus came, lived a perfect life, and died on the cross for you and me. And, one day, he will return to earth and pick up those who are saved. Some people will believe this. Some people will not believe this. Even after he comes back, there will be those who will accept him and he will accept them into the kingdom of heaven. However, there will be those who will deny him to the end, just like the Jewish people did when he died on the cross.

I don't know how to make a person believe in Jesus. Like I said, it took me a long time to accept, and I still don't understand it all. But, I know that my life has become a lot more fulfilled since I began living a life with God, trying to live his truths. And, I know that God has a plan for my life. And, I have both lived in the will of God, and outside of the will of God and I can tell you that to live in the will of God is a lot more pleasant. Also, I can tell you that you can make $200,000 a year on your own outside the will of God, or you can make $30,000 with the will of God, and you will live a lot more comfortable with the $30,000 a year in the will of God. I can also tell you that there is a peace that comes with knowing that you have been honest, and that everything you live for is honest and in the open. Furthermore, there is a peace that comes with knowing that your sins are forgiven because of the life of Christ.

If you don't know Christ tonight, and I have not said anything that touched your heart, I can accept that. Honesty with this is the best answer. But, please get a Bible for your self, and start on page 1 and read the entire book. What I have not convinced you of if you will open your heart to him, he will convince you of. You see, I have a lot of errors, faults, and am not perfect. God is perfect, and he wants you to live the way he had planned. Selah.

At War

I have had no trouble being a United States soldier since becoming a Christian, or before for that matter. The military that I am a part of is for the most part, made up of very honest and Christian men, who want to do the right thing. Like I said earlier, there are a lot of meetings that I have been to in the military that the first words that were spoken were a prayer to God that he would give us the knowledge, wisdom, and understanding to do that which needed to be done.

Our enemy, Al Qaeda, would have the world think we are evil. While we are sitting on our bases trying to sleep at night, they are out trying to plant 155 MM rounds in the dirt to kill innocent US soldiers. As our soldiers drive by these bombs on the way to give citizens of Iraq or Afghanistan aid or food, they blow the bombs up from behind buildings or walls, to kill our soldiers while they hide. A coward's way of warfare. While we do not shoot unless shot at, they openly shoot at us with a sniper from behind buildings or trees. While we are out trying to build new roads and infrastructure for their country, they are out recruiting mentally ill men and women to walk into markets with suicide vests on to blow up innocent civilians, or US Military. Al Qaeda and the Taliban are evil, and we as Americans have to become committed to destroying this evil before it festers like Hitler did. Hitler was one man doing evil work (killing Jews), but look at how many Germans became brainwashed that they were doing right.

And, I know what someone is thinking; if we had not come over here (Iraq or Afghanistan) that we would not be getting shot at. Well, the truth is we don't want to be here. We would rather that Iraq, or Afghanistan or who ever would have a government who was fair to its people, that took care of its suffering and poor, that was not corrupt, and that did not see the future beyond continuing to fight against God's people. If the best the Islamic people can see in their future is always being at war against Israel, then they have a bleak future indeed.

According to a memo from the number 2 man in Al Qaeda in 2006, that is all the Islamic people have to look forward to. Why would God, the almighty, who gave us everything on earth, limit the Islamic people to fighting a war they cannot win?

However, I will give them this. God has sustained them for thousands of years in the middle of the desert with little water or food. Many of these people want peace, and just want to be left alone. Al Qaeda lives in the middle of them not because the people want them there, but because they just want to be left alone. They figure, if we leave them alone, maybe they will leave us alone. It is a good argument, but one that sets us at war with each other for a long time. If Al Qaeda went away, then America would go away. America only wants to do war with those who would attack our own or our allies. But, the Al Qaeda terrorists will always be on the move against our families to kill and maim us because we are Christians. We will always be at war with them.

We, the United States Government, have walked the high road ever since invading Iraq after having the twin towers blown up. And, if Saddam Hueissein did not have anything to do with the blowing up of the towers, he did have massive amounts of yellow cake (nuclear waste material) and chemicals laid up in Baghdad, and Hezbollah training was prevalent here. Very little has ever been put out on this, but the Qa Qa Weapons Facility in Baghdad is large enough to store enough munitions to take over Eastern Europe. And, while by the time Allied Forces came in most of it had disappeared; it went somewhere. Iran? Who knows. All I know is that what ever was there (Qa Qa Weapons Facility) changed the appearance of the earth to where nothing grows, and there are still mounds of mortar, rocket, and other ammunition to be found all over this 3-4 mile facility.

Anyway, we as a country (US) have fought for our freedoms on the defensive up to this point. We have fired only if fired upon. However, after spending two years in Iraq, I have to question if we are doing the right thing. We are allowing a false understanding of a religion to attack us in the name of men. And, what really gets me is that the beginning of the Muslim religion started with them worshipping the same God we did. Allah was the God of Abraham. So, how did men with the beginning of praying to the same God, change the way they thought to where they see fit to blow up Americans. And do you remember, God blessed Abraham for being willing to sacrifice his son, so he spared his son and gave him a lamb. This lamb is the pre-cursor of Jesus. If only we could open your eyes.

We invite thousands of Muslims in the United States each year to study at our Universities, allow them to build mosques in our country, allow them to have access to our health care, allow them to live in our country and buy land if they want. And how are we repaid; we are spit on. Muslims blow up our twin towers. They plot on how they will kidnap and kill our young soldiers, or visitors to their countries. They plan to attack Israel, the basis of our religion, and theirs if they looked deep enough. And they say they are doing it for the God of Israel? They have lost track of who Abraham was.

At this point, I would have to say we (Americans) need to throw down our pitch forks and rakes and repel the invaders. If they choose to kill one of our children, then we should take every one of their students out of the United States and send them home. After all, they create these secret cells to plan terror at night, while they work and make money on our economy during the day. If they were truly blessed in the work they do, why would they hide while they did it. If they were doing Gods work planning on killing the infidels, then they would be in his will. The truth is they are doing evil, and that is why they work in the dark. The truth is, they pray on young men and women with mental disorders, strap waist bombs on them, and then send them off to commit killings in a crowded Baghdad market. This is murder. This is not war. Thou shalt not kill.

If they bomb our cities, we will destroy them completely. We will completely and utterly destroy the remembrance of them from the face of the earth. You say, that is not the Christian thing to do. We have been doing the Christian thing with them for 1000 + years. They don't get it. They don't get that we are trying to live peacefully with them. They don't get that we are trying to help them build better lives for themselves and their families. They don't get that we have given money, time, and countless lives so that they can worship and live with freedoms. And what do they do? They allow Al

Qaeda to live in their back yards. How do they see us as infidels when we have given billions of dollars in aid, food , and water to sustain them and help rebuild their country. And I say this, but I only mean it if it is God's will. If it is God's will, I would ask that we go to war, and end this Muslim-Christian war during our lifetime, so it does not go into my grandchildren's life.

And, to top that off, we went against every principle of warfare since the beginning of time. When troops go to war, they are to live off the country they invade. We should have taken all the oil and all the assets from Iraq and stripped it dry to pay for coming over there. Instead, what did we do, we gave . We gave and gave and gave, and now that we have hurt ourselves through giving to the Iraqis, we continue giving. And, you would think that the Iraqi government would want to repay us by giving us discount oil or other resources. Instead, they take their oil and sell it to Russia or others.

There are many passages in the Bible where it says it is ok to defend oneself. We have lived the turn the other cheek so many times now to where the American cheek has permanent damage. It is time for we, America, to get tired of trying to kill a pig with a fly swatter if it is the will of God. While my anger precludes perhaps that which is right, we need a group of our strongest Christian leaders to meet and pray to God for what to do. What should we do to an enemy that will not stop invading?

Now, some of the facts that relate to this are as follows:

The Fundamentalist Muslims are murdering innocent civilians without provocation in the name of their religion. They place vehicle borne IEDs (bombs) in their markets and along side the roads which kill innocent bystanders.

The Fundamentalist Muslims are teaching their kids to hate those who are Americans or not Muslims.

The Fundamentalist Muslims are training a group of terrorists who, if given the

opportunity, would come inside of our borders and kill our citizens because they do not like us.

Iran, a Fundamentalist nation, has weapons of mass destruction, including more than one facility to create and manufacture nuclear weapons. One facility, near Qom, has an underground Nuclear facility to produce nuclear warheads.

Iran, fights Israel, by supporting Hezbollah. Hezbollah would not even be known if it was not for the money and weapons that Iran gives them. Hezbollah is the face, Iran is the body.

We, as the United States of America, have an obligation to Israel to defend it.

Our money states in God we Trust. We as a nation were born and started as a Christian nation, no matter what you want to believe. Once again, look at the front of most Government building and look for the unfinished stone. Coincidence it was placed on most government buildings? The unsaid meaning of that stone is from both Psalms 118:22 and Matthew 21:42, as well as other places in the Bible, where Jesus states " the stone which the builders rejected, the same has become the head of the corner: this is the Lords doing, and it is marvelous in our eyes."

The best solution to all of this is that the young people of Iran, Pakistan, Syria and Afghanistan see and understand that we want to live in peace with their countries, and have a revolution to start back over again.   Since the beginning of trade, we have sought out goods and services from them. We have wanted free trade, and mutual aid. We have wanted for their citizens to have the freedom to worship their God the way they want to , and to enjoy freedoms as God would intend it. If the young people in these countries could only see that there is a life beyond being paid $50 to plant an IED to blow up an American soldier, or beyond wearing a suicide vest in the market for the possibility to go to heaven with 50 virgins. Is that really in the Koran? What do women get for blowing themselves up? 50 male virgins? Who knows?

Lets reason together.   America does not want to be at war with you. But if you keep threatening our young people and lives, we have no choice. We cannot keep throwing our pearls in the mud with the pigs. As you know, the pigs will eat and trample over everything and soon we will have no pearls left.

As you worship today, I would ask that you pray on your own that God will give you a plan for your life. I would ask that you would pray for our Islamic brothers that they would receive knowledge and understanding. However, I would ask that you as a fellow brother in Christ become fully armed in the knowledge that you may be called upon one day to fight for that by which is right in America. For freedom of worship. For the right to bear arms. For the right to live freely in one of the greatest nations that has ever lived. It was never the government that made America strong, although we have been blessed with a strong central government. It was the individual, who made a living through his own life without ever needing government assistance. It was the embodiment of everything that Harley Davidson, an American owned motorcycle company, existed for.

One argument that is often argued is that American's were not poor in the beginning of America. Yes we were. George Washington, the first President of the United States, had to borrow money to go to be inaugurated as President. He owned a lot of land, but was so poor from speculation to where he had little cash. So were most of the initial men who were there at the beginning. There is nothing wrong with being honest and poor. The problem therein lies when you begin to lust, lie, cheat, steal, to get ahead. It is better to be a poor man with a piece of bread, than a rich man going to Hell.

If you show me someone who lives in America, I will know him or her by their strong independence and freedom of speech. If you show me a true American, you will show me a small business owner who runs his or her own business, who is making a living without depending on any government help, and who is able to sustain others through this vision: John Belk, John D. Rockefeller, Bill Gates, Bruton Smith, Bill Gates, and the list goes on and on. God gave you a mind to do great things. Get up, get moving, and start creating. That is what made America into what it is.

The Atheist

There once was a man who worked for one of the largest banks in America. He had no faith in God. He often laughed at Christians and said often "keep up the good fight." He thought Christians as well as all humans who believed in the true, living God, were a joke.

This man was very organized, and was seemingly very blessed. He rose to a very high position with the bank, and then was offered a high position with the US Government. While at the bank, he found it funny to make account numbers for customers with 666 in it. In fact, he had created over 1 million account numbers with this symbol in it, thinking it was funny. When working for the Government, he was able to set up a computer program that put the number 666 in thousands of Social Security Numbers, State License Tags, Tax Payer ID Numbers, Corporate Identification Numbers, telephone numbers, etc. He was a master of computers, and always believed he could break into anyone's computer and track what they were doing.

For a large government organization, he created a system that tracked every key that any individual ever used on a computer, and was publically praised for his help in fighting Al Qaeda and other terrorists.

Many people who rode down the roads thought, "I see a lot of license tags with 666, but none with 777, or 444, or 111. That is strange." People had the thoughts, but no one ever did anything about it. Also, addresses. "How did so many 666 numbers show up on home addresses?", many people thought but they just thought it was a coincidence.

Everyone forgot that "mysterious, odd, not hurting anything, questionable, and strange" are words people thought about Hitler when he became a Dictator in Germany.

At a future date, that no one knows, the Anti Christ came to power. His system for allowing people to eat, make money, have a job, and basically be marked for service was already in place thanks to the work of this one banker. Humans once again questioned how easy the transition was, because the system was already in place and we all just shrugged our shoulders.

Water passing over a rock does nothing in a day. But over time, it too wears a rock to nothing.

Rebuilding America

"Ask not what your country can do for you. Ask what you can do for your country." I believe these words to be from a speech given by President John Kennedy. It is time we as Christians see again the light. We will not be able to change everyone, but we must come together and change ourselves, and through our words and deeds, perhaps we can change others. There are men that will always be slothful with work; these men I just don't know. Thomas Jefferson once said something to the effect that the fastest way to destroy a country is to make those willing to work pay for those who are not. But, for those of us who can, the time to rebuild is now. We have to accept there always have been and always will be people who are unable and unwilling to work. Get it in your mind you cannot change that. What you can change is yourself and those around you.

We have gotten a huge debt with China. I do not know how it will be repaid during our lifetime, but we need to repay it. If you can, I would ask that each American that can provide $1000 to repay the debt of China. It would take a lot from each of us, but we need to do it. We need to fix this national debt we are in. And the money needs to be collected by a non-profit, non-governmental agency, founded by a successful Christian businessmen, who can give it directly to the Chinese government and pay off our deficit. And, we should expect nothing back from our government for it.

We need to become self dependent. Instead of our minds focusing on how we can get on Social Security, welfare, Medicare, Medicaid, etc. we need to focus on how we can get by without them. Let the weak and poor take these subsidies. If you can, and for as long as you can, take care of yourself only paying taxes, not taking anything from the government. We don't need any of these items if we have strong enough families, and this will take all of you. The only way to truly accomplish this is for families to build large homes, and to have the grandparents, parents, children, and others live under one roof with the focus on taking care of the family. As older people get older, we take care of one another. The world has and will continue to stress placing older people in nursing homes and let Medicare pay for it. Take care of those who cannot take care of themselves without government help.

Next, we need to elect in officials who will once again look at taking care of us. As many of these as possible, I would ask to work for free for the government. We don't want crack heads and hoars in government. We want strong, financially secure, individuals who will serve government without expecting to be served. We don't need scandals, bribery, corruption, loose morals. We need men of character who can guide this great nation past this moral depravity that has become our cornerstone. Don't forget that George Washington was cash poor, but land rich when he was elected to become President. We need strong church leaders to once again take over our government so that we can once again call ourselves one nation under God instead of what we are now, one nation who is going away from God.

I am so tired of hearing that men cannot find work. Men, be like our forefathers. Build things. Start creating something and sell it. Become an entrepreneur. Find the talent that God gave you and start your own business. We have a huge trade deficit every year because we are buying Chinese made goods and services, that could be produced in America. For example, there is a furniture manufacturing ready to begin again. We just need to start small and build. And, people always need their house painted, and yard work done, and builders. Go to work laying bricks as a brick mason and learn a trade. Get out of the computer industry. There are enough of those.

Finally, work hard but don't expect to be a millionaire your first year. Understand that if you work that which is right, if you pray, if you live right, you can live as well on $30000 a year as you have on $200000 a year. Especially if you plant a garden throughout the year.   Do you remember how Jesus fed 5000 people with just a couple of fish and bread. With ourselves we will fail. Through the power of God, anything can be done. American's, and that is what we are, lets start feeding ourselves with no need for government. I know this is not easy if you do not have a job. But, pray and get a focus and work toward where you are led. If you are led to start a small business, then start it.

If you have a farm, grow crops. If you don't intend to use the land, rent it out to someone who will grow things. We need to utilize all the assets that God gave our land. He gave us land, trees, gold, silver, fruit trees, vegetables, cattle, rivers and the ocean full of fish, cotton, salt, technology; the list goes on and on.

In the end, know that it was God who gave us the resources of the land.

It is God who gives all things, and it is he who takes away. Use the gifts and items that God has given you, instead of focusing on what you don't have. America is the land of milk and honey, but you have to milk the cow and invade the bees hive to have it.

Raising Children

If you have children, you have the God given responsibility to discipline them. God says, spare the rod, spoil the child. Children have the responsibility to honor their parents, so that their days may be long. America is one generation away from having citizens with no moral values. Or even yet, they may have negative moral values, not only being immoral, but taking away from those who may try to exude morality. The scale is tilting that way.

Since starting to write, I have been trying to not watch any television except news and sports. I like the Minnesota Vikings this year since Brett Fauve is on it. By the way, they won again yesterday, 10/19/09 and are now (5-0). Miracles continue to happen. But, anyway, yesterday at lunch, I went to eat with a couple of soldiers I work with, and they wanted to sit where the television was in the military dining facility. So, we sit down, and I start eating lunch, and this movie is on where these bad guys are trying to kill a man, a woman, and a child. So, I keep eating, and I am reading a newspaper, and look up and this man and woman are now naked, having sex, and he is having a gun fight, and the baby is just laying there awake on the floor while all of this is going on. Yes, the guy in the movie was so great that he could keep having sex while bad guys were trying to break through windows to kill him, with guns a blazing, and the woman was not focused on the baby or the gun fight, just sex. Our minds are warped from years of such. Our children are growing up with these DVDs in their homes, because their parents are watching them.

America, what are we doing to ourselves? Why are we going to this extreme for entertainment. What ever happened to families sitting around playing monopoly, or going for long walks. How did Hollywood get so far skewed from making Walt Disney movies, to making movies where the hero has adultery while having a gun fight. And all for the sake of entertainment. Who knows? Kids who watch movies like this grow up and think this is how I need to become when I become older.

In Iraq, few people tell the truth. They think that it is alright to tell a "white lie" because it is the way they do business. They have access to black market items that are exact images of items we use in America. They are one of the most corrupt nations in the world because their children are not taught right from wrong. I have not read the entire Koran, but does the Koran not teach any right from wrong, and it is from Abraham? Am I missing something. Is there only darkness and death in the Koran. Is there no light? Children should be taught the importance of telling the truth, and spanked when they lie.

When I first got here, Iraq, I needed to purchase some printer cartridges for the printers that we were using here in country. They were a type of Hewlett Packard printer cartridge, I cannot the exact nomenclature. Well, I used money from a fund we have to purchase such items on the local economy when we cannot get them through the normal Army Supply Channel, which we did. These printer cartridges, after we got them, looked new. They were in a new box, with plastic around them and the instructions were in the box. We put them in the printers, and they did not work. What we later found out were that they were refurbished cartridges, and that you had to put a special code in the printer to make them work. We were eventually able to get the code to work and get the cartridge to work, but they were not the original cartridges. They were refurbished cartridges made just so the user would think they were new. I mean it looked new, even had instructions in the box. And the seller did not tell me they were not new. Is this where we are heading in America. Are we so spun up to not teach right from wrong and morale values in public schools to where we will accept the risk all of our children grow up to be corrupt. Could America in 50 years be voted as the corrupt nation in the world? We have the intelligence to be very corrupt. We as Americans can recreate and steal just about anything. Look at the Madoff Investment scheme and other conniving investors who steal money from older people and live the high life. If we don't step in and save our children, no one else will.

We have some very honest and talented people in America. We have people who invent, who write, who study and find understanding in Science, who create. All of these hard working and honest people are being slighted by the people who will steal, market, and profit off their work. It is like you have two kids in school. One studies all night to pass a math test. The other cheats off the paper of the student who studied all night. Are we, America, ready to accept the cheater as worthy of the same grade as the one who studied all night. Unfortunately, some of America will say, yes.

Wake up. It is God who gave us a mind, a body, a spirit, direction, air to breathe, and freedom. And, he can as easily give it away. If you read in the Old Testament, God put the Israelites in bondage (slavery) in Egypt. Then, God called Moses, who did not want to lead, to get them out. He put them in slavery because they were wicked. If the Israelites would have chosen a leader to get them out of slavery, it would not have been probably Moses, as he was not the best speaker or politically connected. In fact, Moses questioned God when God told him to represent the people. He did not feel worthy or noteworthy enough to lead the Israelites.   He finally talked God into giving him an assistant, Aaron. Moses, who was led by God, inspired by God, and given by God for this purpose, eventually won the freedom of the Israelites and took them into the desert. From the beginning of their freedom, they started to complain. (Some people don't deserve freedom). They did not have water, or they did not have food or they did not have this or that. Freedom is not free. The Israelites could have stayed and ate well in bondage with the Egyptians. But, their destiny was to follow Moses and become free. However, God did not lead them through easy land, such as the Philistines, because "Lest the people repent when they see war and return to Egypt." Exodus 13:17. We need to teach our children to follow God, even when times are tough. He will see you through, in his time frame and according to his will.

Our freedom today is also at a cost. We are getting ready to go through the toughest economic times that this country has seen since the Depression. The homes that have been built throughout the United States that were $500k (+) prior to 2007, are going to drop dramatically in price. The stock market is going to continue functioning, but people are not going to be able to trust the companies to invest because so many Chief Executive Officers have lined their pockets, and lied about profits. Companies like Krispy Kreme Doughnuts, Bank of America, American Insurance Group (AIG), and other publically traded companies will have a hard time pulling in investors because they have had problems in the past being truthful.

We are also getting ready to go through one of the toughest times socially that we have ever seen. We will see a split not between blacks and whites, or other races, but between workers and non-workers.   We will see tension arise as the Democrats continue pushing for subsidized health care, housing, education, and income off the backs of workers who are already working 2-3 jobs to make ends meet. I am white and know of few truly prejudice white people against blacks: but I know a lot of both blacks and whites that are truly prejudice against the welfare system that they work to subsidize. Men and women who work sometimes 2 and 3 jobs to support their families are tired of paying more so others can sit there and do nothing. Children today should be taught the importance of working, and giving without expecting anything in return.

We are getting ready to see our economic debt, to pay for these subsidies, place America in the worst financial shape that we have ever been in. The Bretton-Wood Act, which backed the dollar with gold for many years, will have to be re-enacted to back the US Currency because no one trusts it. We, America, the land of the free and the home of the brave, are about to become a 3rd world country if we don't change. We need to back our scientists and protect their rights to their inventions. We need to take charge of our publically held companies and make them responsible economically and socially. And, we need to tear our clothes, wail, and beg God for forgiveness for the sins that we have done. For we took that by which God gave us and that was good, and corrupted it to the point that we are all confused. We took that which was wrong, and made it right. We took that by which is right, and made it wrong. And until we gain God's forgiveness, he will not heal our land or bless our work. And, this next generation, unless things change, may not even know who God is. We need an awakening in America today. We need families to understand that our futures depend on them being moral and learning as much as possible in school, so they can survive being an honest generation.

On Homosexuality

I truly don't even know why one would preach on this. Why some man would want to stick his penis up some other guys butt; it does not even make logical sense. Or one woman kiss another woman. Besides the grossness of it, God said several times through the Bible that man was not to be with man, but that a man should leave his home, and join with woman, and that the two shall be as one. Also, that women should not work that which is unnatural among themselves. But, since Old Testament times and before, men and women have done this. Just like Al Qaeda, homosexuals want to be smarter than God.

The argument for this is " well I am just attracted to my own sex." Because you feel weird does that make it right. "Well I just felt like killing twelve women." Because you feel like it does that make it right. Well, I just like dating little girls. Does that make it right? Well, I just felt like blowing up a building and murdering innocent people. Just because you feel like doing something does not change what God sees as right and wrong.

In fact, God does not change what he believes is right and wrong. There were several times he changed his opinion about destroying a town when man repented, but the sin is still a sin. If they did not repent, he would not have changed. If you look outside every morning, the sun rises, and in the afternoon, the sun goes down. The moon appears in the evening skies at the level of what it is through the month (i.e. crescent, full, etc.). The seasons change, and every year we have a Spring. The stars align in their constellations, and animals and fish go North and South every year with the seasons. There is a balance of nature. Homosexuality throws the human race off balance. God created for almost every man, a female of generally the same age and race as him as a spouse. It is natural.

You see these married gay people on television. They think they are smarter than what God has created, the natural family. They have gone and married someone of their own sex, and then adopted kids and say they are a "family." Some of them go and get artificially inseminated with a turkey baster shooting sperm in their vagina. Why, do we, think something stupid like that outsmarts God's original plan, which is as natural as the sun rising? Why could you not see what is natural and not. God created us all. Why would any human being think he or she could outsmart his design.

The weirdness goes on elsewhere in the military. Not my unit, as I don't think the gay thing will go well here. Recently a policy came out that said that gays in the military no longer have to abide by don't ask, don't tell. Alright, does that mean that they must ask, and must tell. Do I now have to hear fags in the military saying something like "look at me, look at me, I am Gay, I am Gay." I just don't get the openly gay thing. Are they to wear a special yellow flowered shirt that announces to the world they are gay.   I am hetero sexual. I don't run around the military saying "look at me, I am heterosexual, I am heterosexual. I have a wife and kids." Why do I have to change anything I am doing so some weird man or woman can come out and announce their sexuality. And guess what? The sex they have between themselves is illegal according to most state General Statutes. How can the Army say something is ok that is illegal in most states??

Man argues this just like he argues everything else. Many say, well I just don't believe that is what it says in the Bible. Or, well I know the Bible is against it but I don't care. Somehow, some way, some churches are even condoning gay ministers? Where are they getting this. Is the next step to make serial killers ministers?   Or child molesters?

I think God was as clear as possible in Sodom and Gomorrah. God sent an angel to see what was happening in the town. Two angels arrive, and visit Lot. Men see them enter, believe them to be men, and want to have sex with them. Lot offers them his daughters, because he wants to protect the angels. They refuse, and only want the men (who are really angels in disguise). Lot winds up giving them his concubine. They wind up raping and beating her, and leaving her to die.   The next morning, the Angels tell Lot to get his family, leave Sodom and Gomorrah and don't look back. Sarah looks back and she becomes a pillar of salt. Sodom and Gomorrah is no more.

This could just as easily be San Francisco. Yesterday in the news there was news where a 15 year old girl was repeatedly raped during a homecoming high school football game under the bleachers while fans stood, watched, and some even video taped. (I bet as Lot's Concubine was raped and beat the crowd just stood and watched). When the men were finished, she was left under the bleachers for almost 30 minutes before someone called 911 and reported this incident. Men and women who watched this atrocity (as of now they have found 20) , even video taped it with a cell phone. She was taken to the hospital and is in critical condition. This sounds a lot like Lot's concubine. Out of all the people who stood and watched as 4 men raped her, none stepped in and helped. Do you not think God knows this. We as a society should be ashamed and tear our clothes and wail and ask for forgiveness. Instead, we will remain apathetic because it did not happen to us. We often forget anything until we are at the funeral, and death becomes personal. You remember at the funeral how you ask why we don't get together more. The death of someone we know changes the paradigm of everything. It makes it personal.

Homosexuality in America is also one more thread tearing apart families. I know in our family we have at least one proclaimed homosexual who left home and lives with her partner in Florida. She will not come and visit family because she thinks they will think her lifestyle to be wrong. In fact, she has judged herself worse than her mother and father does, as her mother and father just want her to come home. They love her very much, but yet she does not come home because she believes what she is doing and how she is perceived living (as a homosexual) is wrong. It is wrong. She knows it is. Human beings are the only animals on the planet who blush. God made it that way because we know right from wrong. We have a soul. But, through Christ Jesus, we have forgiveness. Her family forgives her; and just wants her to come home. Do you remember the story of the prodigal son. He wanted his inheritance before his father died. His father gave it to him and he went and spent it all. He wound up having to feed swine to survive. When he finally came to his senses, he went back home and his father welcomed him and cut the fatted cow. That is how God is. You may have left the protection of his home because of sin, but he stands ready to take you back. You just have to ask, and to turn from your evil ways, and sin no more. You will still have lusts, desires, wants, feelings of guilt; you cannot handle them but when you give your life over to God, and ask for your forgiveness of sins through the blood of Jesus, it is done.

America, wake up from this long dream that you are under. Everything is not alright. We are under attack by evil because we have invited it in. We need the country to turn from its past sins, and to ask for forgiveness. For the enemy we fight, is designed to destroy us. We need God in this battle, as we have always needed him. Please, if not for yourself, for others, turn your ways back to that which is right, ask God for forgiveness, and live a correct life. For only through us asking for forgiveness and turning from our evil ways will our land be healed and our children live in peace.

Rasheed's

Once upon a time, there was an Arabic man named Ismaeel Alan. He was a Sunni Muslim. He lived in Baghdad, and had a wonderful family. He had 2 sons, a daughter, and a beautiful wife. Ismaeel owned a small computer company, and sold computers that he fixed himself and guaranteed to work. He did not make a lot of money, but made enough to support his family. He prided himself in doing to others as he would have them to do unto him, and gladly took back any computers that did not work and replaced them or refunded the money. He feared Allah most of all, more than men.

One day, his family was shopping together at a local Rasheed market when a suicide bomber went inside and blew herself up. It killed his wife, his 2 sons, and his daughter. Ismaeel, the man, survived but was badly injured and was in a coma. Two weeks after the coma, Ismaeel woke up, and begins to recover. He is told about his family.

Ismaeel, after about 2 months of therapy, begins to get better. He has had time over the last several weeks to read the Koran himself, and to spend time with Allah, the all knowing. He cannot help but see that the individuals who are spreading Islam with the false doctrine must be stopped. He knows the truth about Abraham, and that God spared his son from being the sacrifice on Mt Moriah. He knows Allah would have no part of his family being killed for a bunch of thugs trying to spread their political agenda.

Ismaeel is not the smartest man. He had graduated from 7th grade but had a limited education. He, however knew he must make a difference in this world, for his family's sake. He discovers who was responsible for killing his family. It was a group of young people who were indoctrinated into the group Al Qaeda, and were followers of a group from Ibrahaim Al Ghaberri. The girl who blew herself up in the market was retarded, and Al Qaeda had paid her parents $300 to allow them to use her. He knows he must act against this evil.

Ismaeel begins to pray and ask for Allah's help. He is soon blessed with an arms dealer who provides him with 2 grenades and 3 x 155 rounds for $175 in Baghdad.

Ismaeel watches the home of Ibrahaim Al Ghaberri. He sees the young men coming by his home every night around 11pm.   He notices that no one watches the home around 4am. Therefore, at 4 am that morning, he takes the 3 x 155 rounds that he has and buries them around Ibrahaims home, with one wire connecting all 3 rounds to a battery.   He has a cell phone that he uses as a detonator. He learned how to wire everything from a website he googled.

Ismaeel is tired after planting the bombs. He goes home and tries to sleep, but between the heat and the constant thoughts of his family, he has trouble sleeping. As always,   he winds up crying himself to a sleep that does not rest,   but one that passes the time. At 3pm the same day, he wakes back up. He is still tired, but makes some tea and eats some left over goat's cheese. He thinks about what he had to do that night.

At 9 pm that night, Ismaeel shows back up near Ibrahaim Al Ghaberris home, hiding behind a building. He prays. He has his cell phone ready.   At 11pm, about 25 of the men who work for Ibrahaim show up at his house.   They are drinking some type of alcohol, and are laughing loud. One of them is showing off a new gun that he had. Ismaeel dials the cell phone number. The 155 rounds detonate. The bombs blow up the house and everything around it. Ismaeel is surprised at how loud the rounds are. Ibrahaims house and everything in it disintegrates. Ismaeel feels better.

The story of what Ismaeel has done spreads around the country side quickly. He gains notoriety, as the people of Baghdad are tired of war. They did not like the Americans being in their country, but at the same time they do not like the Al Qaeda blowing up families to further their agenda, especially using a retarded person. Many people gather around Ismaeel. One man, Oman Achmed, a former Baath Party Member, talks Ismaeel into running for public office, as the President of Iraq. Ismaeel prays about it, and decides he wants to do the right thing for the people of Iraq. He runs for office and wins the election with the help of Oman.

Ismaeel's first job as President is to focus his government on security. He already has had many death threats on his life from Al Qaeda, and stays within his security compound except for meetings due to these death threats. He begins to understand that the only way to defeat Al Qaeda is to fight them as they fought his family. He begins to recruit former individuals who planted IEDs and pays them $200 for each bomb they successfully plant that kills an Al Qaeda member. Soon, he has over 3,000 members on his payroll, fighting Al Qaeda. Al Qaeda within 3 months is completely wiped out of Iraq, or any members who remain stay underground because they are afraid of Ismaeel.

Soon, for the first time in many years, the country is able to focus on rebuilding the economy. Ismaeel recruits many of the individuals who helped him defeat Al Qaeda to become his intelligence unit for his government. He soon has viable intelligence flowing into his headquarters on who is a threat. He does not put up with the threat, and defeats the snake (Al Qaeda) each time it tries to come back out of the hole.

One of the first signs of the new Iraq economy is the investment that foreigners make inside of Baghdad. Ismaeel takes an unprecedented step and takes part of the revenues from the oil refineries and gives it as a dividend to citizens who are registered and have an address in Iraq, and a valid identification. By paying the citizens a dividend, he is also able to obtain validity on who should be in Iraq and who should not. Within 2 years, he is able with the help of Police to detain or export all peoples found within the boundary of Iraq who do not have a valid identification card.   Terrorist bombings during this year also go down to 1, which was planted in a Water Treatment facility to stop the progress he was making on providing clean drinking water.

He also used oil revenues to help pay for electrical projects throughout Iraq and water projects. He takes no money for himself, but gives it all back to the people of Iraq. During the 2nd election, Ismaeel is unanimously elected as the President. Within the 4 years of Ismaeel's tenure, he is able to help rebuild the country from a war torn country, to one of growing economic performance. Ismaeel wins the Nobel Peace Prize for his efforts in creating peace in Iraq, something that the United States and other countries have never been able to do, no matter how much money and effort they put in there.

Many surrounding countries, take note and elect independent candidates to office.

Pakistan, who has been fighting the Taliban, elects Joseph Jaban as President. He takes his office just like Ismaeel. He refuses to take a salary, and gives the revenues of the state back to the people of the state. He creates the first Pakistani Intelligence Service designed just to rid the country of Taliban and Al Qaeda fighters. Soon Pakistan becomes profitable as a country and the children there begin to go back to school. Any members of the Taliban go into hiding, as they are seen as the snake that they are. He fights them using the same techniques that they use: he places IEDs outside of their homes, their cars, and their mountain caves.

During the year 2012, the world economy picks back up again. People have confidence in what is happening, and believe that the right people are in office. Most of the terrorists from Iraq, Afghanistan, Syria, Pakistan, and other Middle Eastern countries move into Somalia and join in with the Pirates.

In June 2012, the United States and its allies invade Somalia. They take over the country completely within 38 hours. They build bases throughout the country, much like they had in Iraq. During the first year of their occupation, they train the people on how to have fair elections. In the Fall of 2013, the first election is held. Owerio Mojweor is elected as the President of Somalia. He has studied the techniques of Ismaeel Alan of Iraq, Joseph Jabaan from Pakistan, and others and their techniques for building a stable, peaceful government in a minimum amount of time. He begins by hiring the head of an intelligence agency. Soon, he is able to hire citizens of Somalia to plant IEDs in the homes and other places to take out the snakes. By 2015, Somalia becomes one of the top 30 places to live in the world. Owerio, his wife Sarah, and his two children are able to walk down the road without bodyguards during the May Day Parade in 2015. He feels completely safe and secure.

In the United States, the Dow Jones Industrial Average in 2015 goes over 15000 for the first time ever. Fuel Prices on average are at $1.54 a gallon. The unemployment rate goes down to 4.5%, with the highest per capita income since 1994. Life is good, and it is owed to one man, Ismaeel Alan, who although he lost his family, was blessed with the knowledge and understanding necessary to change the world.

Conclusion

One might ask, what is the bottom line. Well, what I want to say is that I would like to motivate men to work harder, and America to go back to God, and for world peace, and for businesses and government everywhere to be honest and tell the truth, for peace in Jerusalem, for adequate food and water for all human beings on earth; and these are all things I want. But these, as ideal as they sound, are shallow. The true desire, and the one that I fight daily to stay in touch with, is that the important thing is that God's will be done. Whether it is through peace, war, famine, abundance, drought, poverty, wealth. Once again, lets look at Jesus prayer, which actually sums up this dilemma:

Our father, who art in heaven, hallowed be thy name, thy kingdom come, thy will be done, on the earth as it is in heaven, give us this day , our daily bread, and forgive us our trespasses, as we forgive those who trespass against us, and lead us not into temptation, but deliver us from evil, for thine is the kingdom, the power and the glory, forever.

This, no matter how much my soul wants things or blessings, is why we live. For God's will. When we are in it, it is like paddling a boat down river. When we do things against it, it is like paddling a boat up a water fall. Grow where you are planted, and don't move unless you are moved by God. For ultimately, his will be done.

   And, no matter how smart Steven Hawkins and other atheist authors are, they can never answer where the first matter came from. Or, how did Isaiah know the world was round when everyone else was talking about the earth being flat. Or, where did the first animal come from. Why do humans blush?

   Finally, ask for forgiveness of sins and walk the plumbline that God has given us in the Bible for our lives. Your life will not be easy, as it was not for Adam and Eve after they sinnned. But, if you trust God, you may not always have what you want, but you will always have what you need.

It does not have to be public, but it does need to be real, honest relationship between yourself and God. And, accept Jesus as the free gift from God for your salvation.

May God bless you, your family, and the United States of America.